MW01715205

THE BUSINESS PROCESS MANAGEMENT GUIDEBOOK

AN INTEGRATED ENTERPRISE EXCELLENCE

BPM SYSTEM

Forrest W. Breyfogle III

President and CEO
Smarter Solutions, Inc.
Forrest@SmarterSolutions.com
www.SmarterSolutions.com
Austin, Texas

The Business Process Management Guidebook: An Integrated Enterprise Excellence BPM System

Published by
Citius Publishing Inc.
www.citiuspublishing.com

For additional information and application of the concepts in this book, contact Smarter Solution, Inc. at: info@smartersolutions.com, www.smartersolutions.com, or 512-918-0280.

ISBN: 978-0-9829231-1-5

Manufactured in the United States of America

10 9 8 7 6 5 4 3 2

CONTENTS

1

Why I Wrote This Book and How You Can Benefit from It

Over the years some companies have been very successful and others not so successful; however, even the best-performing companies typically have difficulty sustaining their performance, especially when there are leadership changes.

To illustrate this point, consider how Apple's performance degraded after Steve Jobs left the company in the 1980's but turned around when he returned in the 1990's. It is scary to me that the success of a company should be so closely tied to the brilliance of one or a few executives. What happens if the decision-making executive is wrong or leaves the company? In an extreme case, the company could have difficulty surviving. Organizations are subjecting themselves to high risk when they depend so much on the brilliance of one or a few executives, especially since the complexities of the business world are continually increasing, which makes decision making more difficult.

Individual executives might feel good about having so much decision-making authority and career success. However, they can at the same time be feeling the stress and concern about what would happen if key decision makers in the organization were "run over by a bus" or decided to leave the company.

Many possess these concerns. The question is: what should be done differently to confront these exposures head on? My answer is that organizations need to incorporate an *"orchestrated business process management (BPM) system"* that moves them toward achieving the 3Rs of business; i.e., everyone doing the Right things, and doing them Right, at the Right time.

A goal of this system needs to be that activities are orchestrated so that everyone in the organization moves in the same direction toward benefiting the enterprise as a whole. This system needs to be process-based, break down silos, be data-driven, and must eliminate playing games with the numbers. This system needs to help executives create a long-lasting infrastructure that remains after they decide to move on.

Stephen Covey in his book *Seven Habits of Highly Successful People* (Covey, 2004) describes how someone might use a map to determine how to travel to some other location in Chicago; however, if this person were erroneously given a map of Detroit, he/she would have much frustration, no matter what his/her attitude and beliefs are. Similarly, organizations need a structured roadmap for implementing BPM. Otherwise, their organizations too can experience much frustration and disappointment in attempting to implement BPM, no matter how many effective soft skills are possessed by their personnel.

This book provides a high-level roadmap for implementing BPM which addresses these needs. This directional guide will be referred to as Integrated Enterprise Excellence (IEE) BPM Enterprise Process Management, or IEE BPM/EPM. This roadmap provides a system so that organizations can effectively implement BPM. Organizations can immediately benefit from a portion of the described business process management system and later grow into more/all attributes of this methodology over time.

If you are interested in more application details of the described system, many references are given to the following three references throughout this book: ABPMP BPM CBOK®, *IEE Volume II*, and *IEE Volume III*. The reference section at the end of this book provides details about these books and other referenced sources. The symbols and glossary section near the end of this book also can be used to help you with the understanding of unfamiliar terms.

The book, *Built to Last: Successful Habits of Visionary Companies* by James Collins and Jerry Porras (Collins and Porras, 2004), conceptualized the concept BHAG, which stands for Big Hairy Audacious Goal. My BHAG is that in addition to companies and other organizations benefiting from the concepts in the book, business schools will start to include some of the described methodologies in their curriculum so that organizations throughout the globe can see how they can benefit from the described techniques.

Let's now see how you might benefit from this book by first having you consider a situation that you can most relate to. You should keep in mind in this selection process that the described scenarios and book topics make reference primarily to business applications and benefits; however, the techniques apply equally well to government, non-profits, and other non-business entities.

1.1 Which Scenario Best Describes You?

Select one of the following scenarios, which most closely describe your situation. I will later, in Chapter 21, provide my thoughts on what might be done for each of these situations.

1. You have been selected to revive the financials of a company as its new CEO. You are certain that the company's business management system needs to be improved, but you are not sure what would be the best alternative.

2. You are an executive who reports to the CEO of a company that is doing well; however, you are concerned that the competition may soon be eroding your market share.

3. You are working in a company that has declining financials, and you believe something should be done differently in the business.
4. You are working in a company that is doing well, but there are few performance measures and standard operating procedures. Meetings don't seem to address the real issues, and things are chaotic. You believe that more systems and standard operating procedures are needed.
5. You have been selected to lead a newly-formed process improvement function.
6. You have been selected to lead a BPM deployment.
7. Your BPM deployment is focusing first on process automation; however, you believe that more could be done with the management system supporting the BPM deployment so that the overall financials benefit.

Do you believe that you have a solid approach that has a high probability of success for the working environment that you selected? Do you think that there might be a better way than the approach you chose for your selection? Are you interested in considering a structured system approach that could be used to address all the above challenges? If you would like to consider a somewhat different approach to resolve the above challenges, this book is for you.

This book provides the structure to achieve the desired organizational attributes that are described in various business-management and personal-improvement books. For example:

- The learning organization concept was coined through the work and research of Peter Senge and his colleagues in the book, *The Fifth Discipline* (Senge, 1990). A learning approach to organizational behavior encourages a shift to a more interconnected way of thinking.

- "Begin with the End in Mind" is a phrase coined by Stephen Covey as habit two in his book *Seven Habits of Highly Effective People* (Covey, 2004).

This book describes the structure of how an enterprise can efficiently and effectively compile and share information so that it can become a learning organization. Some readers might think that the described techniques are too difficult for them to incorporate in their company now; hence, they might conclude that their organization needs to start with a simpler approach. I disagree. The complexity of business is growing, and organizations need to have a system that addresses these needs. To have long-lasting success, organizations need to initiate their journey for addressing all the above listed scenarios with a begin-with-the-end-in-mind approach.

Near the end of this book, in Section 23.1, some start-small-then-grow-bigger approaches will be described. I hope that this section will give you some ideas on how to apply the methodologies described in this book immediately.

1.2 Why Use a BPM/EPM Implementation Roadmap?

Many books provide information about the standardization of work processes; however, little is discussed about the standardization of a business management system that could be used in various work environments. This book will describe a roadmap for overcoming this omission. Techniques described in this book can be used to achieve standardization through integration of business process management (BPM) and enterprise process management (EPM).

Implementing business process management (BPM) guidelines can be found in many sources, but the methods to ensure that the BPM effort aligns with your strategic needs are not so obvious. It is assumed that the business system is up to the task of maintaining this strategic alignment, even though most organizations admit that they struggle keeping their management projects aligned.

This book will walk through a series of methods and simple tools that will allow any organization to maintain a strong strategic alignment in its BPM effort along with the alignment of nearly every other management initiative. Through the reading of this book, you can find out how easily this can be done. By the end of this book, you will feel ready to initiate the building of this alignment yourself.

Who should read this book? Business leaders, BPM program managers, improvement program managers, and people responsible for activities that are expected to maintain a tight alignment to their strategic plan.

Take-aways from this book include:

- Appreciate the importance of creating a business system for executing BPM.
- Understand the importance of performance reporting to maintaining strategic alignment.
- Recognize how BPM and other metrics can be used to drive new strategies that improve financial performance.
- Understand how to have an alignment of corporate governance and BPM.

1.3 Book's References

To help you apply the concepts in this book, references will be made to the following books with the noted abbreviated titles. Copies of these books can be obtained through book retailers such as www.amazon.com. Books can also be obtained at a discounted price through www.smartersolutions.com.

- *ABPMP BPM CBOK®* (Association of Business Process Management Professionals 2009)
- *IEE Volume II* (Breyfogle 2008a)
- *IEE Volume III* (Breyfogle 2008b)

1.4 Where to Start When Reading This Book

ABPMP BPM CBOK® makes reference to other programs such as Lean Six Sigma and Total Quality Management (TQM) when the discussion of process improvement arises for a BPM deployment. However, I believe that when most organizations undertake BPM, they desire to improve the enterprise as a whole through the systematic documentation, evaluation, regular assessment, and automation of processes. Because of this anticipated objective, I will mention and describe how you can structurally integrate process improvement efforts in an EPM/BPM deployment.

In addition, I chose to first cover the topic of EPM since an initial big-picture view of an organization can provide addition insight to where focus should be given so that the BPM deployment is most beneficial to the organization's "big picture." However, there is nothing wrong with you selecting to start with the later BPM chapters and then read the earlier EPM chapters. The following basic book layout might help you determine where you would like to start:

- General topics, Chapters 1 – 6
- EPM specific, Chapters 7 – 11
- BPM specific, Chapters 12 – 16
- General topics, Chapters 17 – 23

2

Benefiting from BPM/EPM Integration and the Avoidance of BPM Implementation Risks

Gartner provides this definition: "Business process management (BPM) is a management discipline that treats business processes as assets that directly contribute to enterprise performance by driving operational excellence and business agility." These sound great, but are their risks to you and your organization to transition from your current process management system to a BPM system? Yes, there are. Later, I will share my thoughts about these risks, but for now I will include more Gartner statements.

Gartner goes on to say the following about the key essential elements of BPM:

- Comprehending processes through business process modeling for visualization
- Evaluating process performance through attention to the right process metrics

- Generating options for performance improvements through process analysis
- Gaining the willingness to change the processes from the stakeholders involved

The more of these elements which are not currently embraced in your organization the higher levels of risk that you have in a BPM deployment of not succeeding. That is a lot of change to drive into many organizations.

The Association of Business Process Management Professionals (ABPMP) identifies the components of a successful BPM program, as those shown in Figure 2.1.

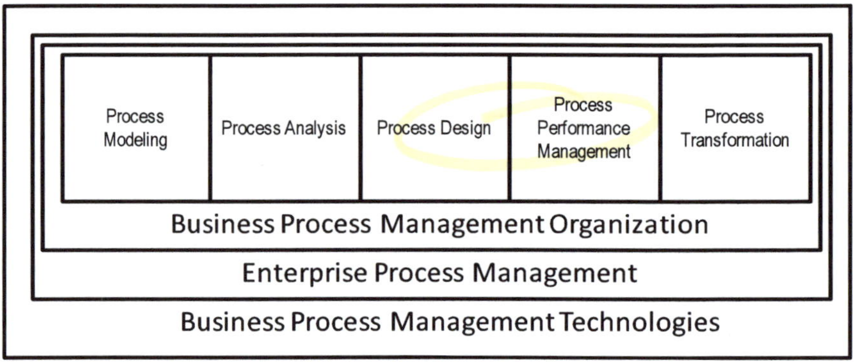

Figure 2.1: BPM CBOK® Organization (*ABPMP BPM CBOK®*)

2.1 BPM Critical Success Factors

An *ABPMP BPM CBOK®* listing of BPM critical success factors is:

1. Define corporate-wide business process value chains and leadership
2. Measure process chain performance
3. Institutionalize practices
4. Standardize business processes

This book will provide a roadmap for accomplishing all these BPM critical success factors. This list will be revisited later in Section 12.3 with the inclusion of a description how this book's described implementation approach addresses each success factor.

If we believe what an association of BPM professionals states, the introduction of BPM is much more complicated than identifying a BPM software suite to buy; it will also require many changes throughout the organizational management. Is there risk in proposing all of these changes? Again, yes there are. Now let's examine some of those risks.

2.2 Risks in a BPM Implementation

If you initiate a business initiative to introduce BPM methods into your organization, there are risks to your business and to you as a leader or initiative participant. To illustrate this point, consider that a BPM deployment is not completed because of culture or other business issues and then disappears over time. The initial BPM deployment risks to you and your organization were:

- Risk 1: Business loss of resources and money that will not be recovered.
- Risk 2: Personal loss of influence and respect for the deployment's leaders. You, as a deployment leader, could lose your job if the business financial loss is high enough.

How much risk are you willing to accept? Reduce your risk through a more thoughtful preparation and deployment of BPM concepts before committing to an expensive IT software solution, which seems so perfect in the marketing materials. Read on to find out how to be more thoughtful in your implementation.

2.3 Benefits and Challenges of Implementing BPM

Why should an organization implement BPM?

- Management-through-processes can help to improve the company's performance in a more and more complex and ever-changing environment. (Thiault 2012)
- Organizations gain higher customer satisfaction, product quality, delivery speed, and time-to-market speed. (Kohlbacher 2009)
- Management of company performance through processes. (Scheer 2007)

Organizations can use BPM as an initiative to move their business forward through the

- Standardization of management practices
- Workflow automation
- Customer experience improvement
- Improved efficiencies
- Reduced non-conformances

All businesses should want these benefits; however, with BPM, as with other business change, there are risks. Common BPM company deployment business risks include wasted expense (software and IT), wasted labor and training, similar process efficiencies after two years, and another "program of the month" implementation. There are also personal risks for the person who is stimulating the change, which include reputation, continued employment, and future influence.

Because of these risks, an individual or organization may choose to do nothing; however, there are risks with that choice, too. Taking no action could lead to a loss in company competitiveness and/or the loss of one's job; however, if a BPM implementation is done right, it can benefit not only the company but also the career of the person who initiates the change.

2.4 Giving Them What Is Needed

BPM alone can offer benefits in an organization; however, often these benefits are in silos that don't positively impact the enterprise as a whole. What is needed is a system for integrating BPM with Enterprise Process Management (EPM). Integrated Enterprise Excellence (IEE) provides such a system for a BPM/EPM implementation.

This BPM/EPM system provides selected checks and balances that will stay in place regardless of management continuity, changes in competitive conditions, or the economic climate. This BPM/EPM system:

- Prevents the organization from executing projects that may be counterproductive.
- Ensures that the BPM efforts support the strategic needs of the organization.
- Eliminates the chance that a newly-automated process does not have the management system required to ensure proper execution.
- Makes sure that your processes are not dependent on a few individuals for success.

This BPM/EPM methodology provides a no-nonsense performance measurement scorecard that serves as an enterprise-wide beacon for orchestrating improvement and innovative efforts so that profitability increases.

2.5 BPM Is Not Only Process Automation

To reiterate, often organizations undertake BPM following the direction of an IT solutions provider who emphasizes process automation. Process automation can be an important aspect of BPM; however, effort needs to be expended to create an effective BPM/EPM integration so that the enterprise as a whole benefits. This book presents a process for an effective implementation and integration of

BPM/EPM where process automation is undertaken so that the enterprise as a whole benefits.

Summary

It is very unusual for a company to have sole ownership of a market. Most companies are striving to hold onto their market share when there is a daily increase in competition.

Individuals and organizations cannot afford to sit still and hope for the best. If the status quo is maintained, they will soon find that the competition is taking away all their business. Organizations need a wise implementation of BPM which structurally leads them to improved productivity, improved flexibility, and improved decision-making so that the enterprise as a whole benefits. Such a system will be described in the on-going chapters.

3

Components of BPM and Their Usage

If we were to examine BPM books and articles, we would find that there are a many differing recommendations for an organization that is considering BPM use.

BPM can offer:

- Documentation and improvement of existing processes.
- Standardization of process execution.
- Enhanced financial decision making.
- Business rules development.

How BPM focus areas are determined:

- Evaluating your company needs.
- Analyzing current business to determine what processes to improve so that the greatest return on investment (ROI) is achieved.

- Identifying which processes are creating customer dissatisfaction issues, which would then be resolved.

The components of BPM architecture may include:

- User interfaces.
- Management dashboards.
- Repository of process descriptions and policies.
- Definition and tracking of key process indicators (KPIs).
- Process simulation.
- Automation and improvement of decision making.
- Business events processes.
- Business rule management system (BRMS) throughout the enterprise for decision-making logic.
- Business events processing (BEP), which addresses whole-enterprise events processing.
- Use of analytics for decision management solution.
- Creation of models that represent the relationships between the inputs and outputs of a process.
- BPM integration with enterprise process management (EPM).

3.1 A System for Integrating BPM with EPM

All of the BPM aspects described in the previous section are good, but what seems to be lacking in the BPM literature is a system for orchestrating the how-tos of implementation. This issue is addressed when BPM is implemented following the Integrated Enterprise Excellence (IEE) system roadmap, as shown in Figure 3.1 and described in this book.

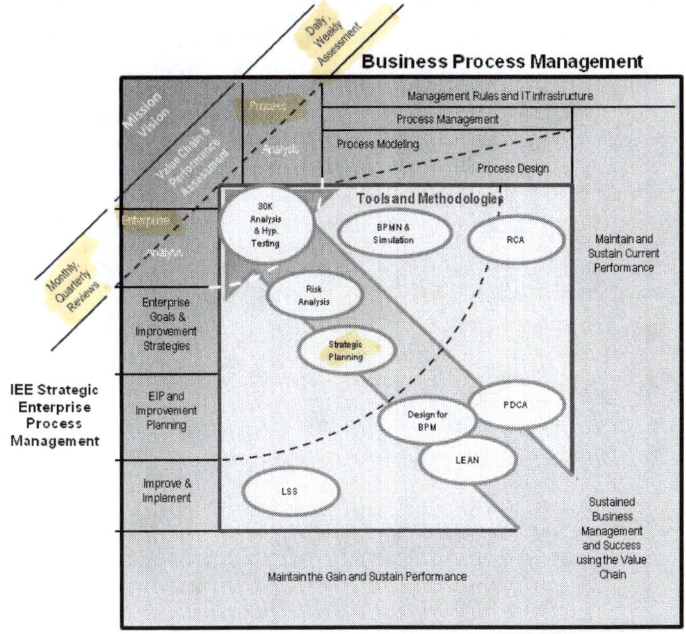

Figure 3.1: IEE Roadmap for integrating BPM and EPM.

A summary of the aspects in Figure 3.1 is:

- The upper left corner describes how a BPM/EPM implementation need should flow out of the organization's vision and mission.
- The next category of a BPM/EPM implementation shown in the upper left corner is "value chain and performance assessment." Through an extension of Porter's value chain (Porter 1985), the IEE value chain provides a description of what an organization does and how it measures its performance.
- Next there is a split in the flow and use of the data provided in the organizational value chain and performance assessment

step. The top horizontal branch of the figure shows the path for the process analysis aspects of a BPM implementation, while the vertical figure's branch addresses the analysis and other activities of the enterprise analysis of EPM system.

- Both paths then combine in the lower right representing the sustaining business success when both paths are emphasized.

EPM execution (vertical split on the left)

- Realistic financial goals are established with a timeline for achievement.
- An analysis of the enterprise as a whole can lead to the establishment or adjustment of enterprise rules that are managed through the IEE value chain.
- Targeted analytically/innovatively-determined strategies are created with an alignment to organizational financial needs and objectives.
- These strategies result in targeted operational value-chain performance goals, whenever possible, where process owners are asking or demanding for the creation and execution of improvement projects that benefit their performance numbers.
- Successful improvement project completion improves the process in an organizational value chain, which results in operational metric improvements that positively impact the enterprise as a whole.
- Controls are established in the organizational value chain to "Maintain the gain and sustain performance" (lower portion of the figure).
- The lower right corner of the figure highlights "Sustain Business Management and Success using the IEE value chain," where the arrow through the graph loops back to enterprise analysis in a Dr. Edwards Deming plan-do-check-act (PDCA)

(Deming 1986) improvement mode for the enterprise as a whole.

BPM execution (horizontal split on the top), which includes the BPM components described in the Figure 3.1 where:

- IT automation of processes is determined from an EPM analysis so that the enterprise as a whole benefits.
- Process modeling is used both to assess implementation risks of new process designs and to optimize processes.
- Design of processes so that they are most effective when implemented.
- IT infrastructure creation, which includes implementation of the IEE value chain with automatic performance data updates, that can readily be accessed by all who have authorization.
- Day-to-day management of processes using the IEE value chain (See *IEE Volume II*, Section 4.5).
- Systematic approach to "Maintain and sustain current performance."
- The lower right corner of the figure highlights "Sustain Business Management and Success using the IEE value chain," where the arrow through the graph loops back to process analysis in a Dr. Edwards Deming plan-do-check-act (PDCA) improvement process mode for operational processes.

The approximate time sequence of potential tool applications in the described IEE BPM/EPM structure is shown as oblong circles in the graphic.

3.2 More Information About BPM/EPM Integration

- IEE value chain creation and performance reporting: *IEE Volume II*, Chapter 7
- EPM implementation: *IEE Volume II*, Chaps. 6 – 14

3.3 Next Topics

What we need to understand about each work process when applying BPM:

Measurements: Use measurement tracking tools in EPM to monitor performance, which provides insight to whether the process is adequate and to know what BPM did to make it better.

Process workflow effectiveness: Many organizations perform a deep dive or process validation to ensure that they do not create a new process that includes all the current day inefficiencies. BPM methods recommend a Lean Six Sigma, Lean, PDCA, or other methods both to improve prior to BPM application and to improve the process later if the automated workflow performance is inadequate.

Rules: Develop process management rules and verify their adequacy before applying the BPM automation and simulation tools. The clear understanding and evaluation of the process management rules prior to BPM application will ensure a good final process.

Process design: New processes need to have efficient and effective workflows that incorporate meaningful specification and integrate effectively with other processes.

Process analysis and modeling: Develop a process analysis and modeling competency to ensure that the new process will perform well as the business grows and as problems arise. Analysis and modeling will ensure that the process you create will be robust to known and many unknown future events.

Process management plan: A robust process management plan should be built to ensure that the identified process metrics are adequate to manage the process. The goal of BPM is either to automate the process execution based on performance metrics or to provide the process users the ability to manage the process based on the performance metrics. If you do not work to develop the right set of metrics, you may still end up with an inefficient automated process.

Process automation: Now consider the IT solution that will fulfill your needs. The information provided to the BPM software team will ensure that they develop a process that will lead the business to greater success.

An IEE integration of EPM with BPM provides:

1. A system for managing the business with multiple processes using effective scorecards and action plans. With this approach, business processes are kept in alignment with the strategic organizational needs using an IEE value chain.
2. An enterprise analysis process is used to identify performance gaps and focus areas that lead to whole-system success.
3. Implementation of a robust improvement methodology so that timely gains are achieved in overall enterprise performance.

4

Foundation for an IEE BPM/EPM System

Organizations gain much when they systematically build from a foundation that begins with a description of why they are in business. Vision and mission statements provide the vehicle for netting out this organizational why.

The next step in building a solid organizational foundation is a description of both what is being done in their processes relative to achievement of this business why and the measurements that assess how well these operational processes are performing. An effective vehicle for communicating this information is an enhancement to the Porter's value chain (Porter 1985), which I will refer to as the IEE value chain and describe later in this chapter.

The IEE value chain provides a description of what is being done and how well the process measurements are performing. This foundation can provide much insight both to what can be done at the local level to effectively manage operational processes and to determine at the enterprise level where strategic efforts should give focus so that the company's overall vision and mission is better achieved.

How a company's vision/mission and its IEE value chain fit within the overall IEE BPM/EPM system roadmap is highlighted in Figure 4.1.

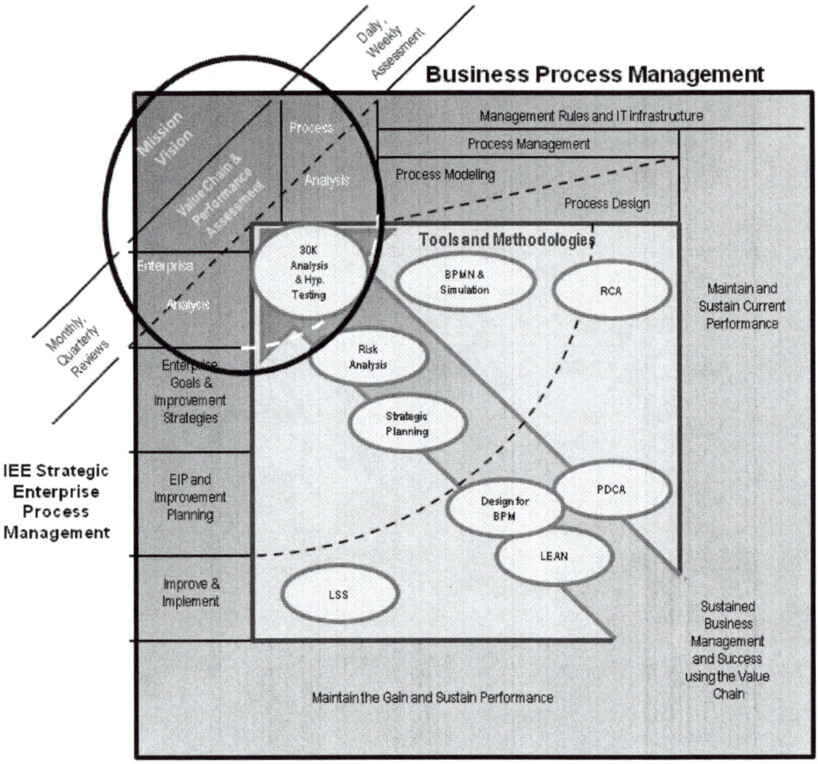

Figure 4.1: Highlighting aspects of the IEE BPM/EPM roadmap.

4.1 Vision and Mission

The vision statement of an organization describes the expected benefits to customers, employees, shareholders and/or society. A vision statement is brief, catchy, inspirational, and believable and serves as a rallying point that clearly states what the organization must become, allowing for execution flexibility.

The Fifth Discipline (Senge 1990) describes the importance of organizations having a shared vision. A shared vision is a force in people's hearts, which has a force of impressive power. The vision might be inspired by an idea, but once it goes further, it creates a sense of commonality that permeates the organization and gives coherence to diverse activities. Senge states that a shared vision is vital for the learning organization because it provides the focus and energy for learning.

A mission statement is a descriptor of why an organization exists and its business intent. As a charter, the mission identifies fundamental customer and market needs that are to be fulfilled. Missions can be created to describe existence purpose not only for the corporate level but also for the organizational level. Mission statements should identify our customers, their needs, offered products/services, and success performance measurements. Missions should be short and memorable to such an extent that people can recite their mission.

As an example, the Coca-cola website (http://www.coca-colacompany.com/our-company/mission-vision-values) states that their corporate mission and vision statements are:

Our Mission

Our Roadmap starts with our mission, which is enduring. It declares our purpose as a company and serves as the standard against which we weigh our actions and decisions.

- To refresh the world...
- To inspire moments of optimism and happiness...
- To create value and make a difference.

Our Vision

Our vision serves as the framework for our Roadmap and guides every aspect of our business by describing what we need to accomplish in order to continue achieving sustainable, quality growth.

- People: Be a great place to work where people are inspired to be the best they can be.
- Portfolio: Bring to the world a portfolio of quality beverage brands that anticipate and satisfy people's desires and needs.
- Partners: Nurture a winning network of customers and suppliers; together we create mutual, enduring value.
- Planet: Be a responsible citizen that makes a difference by helping build and support sustainable communities.
- Profit: Maximize long-term return to shareowners while being mindful of our overall responsibilities.
- Productivity: Be a highly effective, lean and fast-moving organization

---

Let's next discuss how an organizational value chain can effectively describe and communicate what it is doing relative to an alignment of its vision and mission statements.

4.2 Traditional Porter's Value Chain

Porter (Porter 1985) states that a company's value chain is a system of interdependent activities which are connected by linkages. With the Porter value chain model, a company's value activities fall into nine generic categories, which are subdivided into primary and support activities.

Primary activities in a Porter's value chain are those involved in the physical product creation, its marketing and buyer delivery, and support/servicing after the sale. Porter's value chain contains five primary activities: inbound logistics, operations, outbound logistics, marketing/sales, services.

Support activities provide the inputs and infrastructure that allow the primary activities to occur. Every activity employs the three activities of human resource management, technology development, and procurement.

The ninth and final activity of a Porter's value chain is firm infrastructure, which is considered a support activity. Firm infrastructure, which includes such functions as general management, legal work, and accounting, supports the entire chain.

Within each of these generic categories, a company will perform a number of discrete activities, depending on the particular business.

Linkages exist when the way in which one activity is performed affects the cost or effectiveness of other activities. Linkages also require activities to be coordinated. On-time delivery requires that operations, outbound logistics, and service activities should function smoothly together.

4.3 Enhancement of Porter's Value Chain

The IEE value chain is an enhancement to Porter's value chain. All primary and support activities listed for a Porter's value chain should be addressed when creating an organizational IEE value chain. It is most beneficial when formulating an IEE value chain to start at the enterprise level and work downward, creating clickable drill downs and linkages throughout the organization. A clickable IEE value chain can provide timely access to information so that people can better perform their jobs throughout the organization.

Figure 4.2 illustrates a high-level value chain function for a hospital, where the primary activities are connected with an arrow, and support activities are shown as non-attached rectangular boxes. Figure 4.3 illustrates a drilldown of the high-level IEE value chain's function to its procedures and documentation.

With the IEE value chain, organizations have the flexibility of listing high-level primary and support activities or functions for the business, where each of these functions has an owner who is responsible for the execution of the processes for his/her function. The IEE value chain documents value-added, handoff, and control activities of the business.

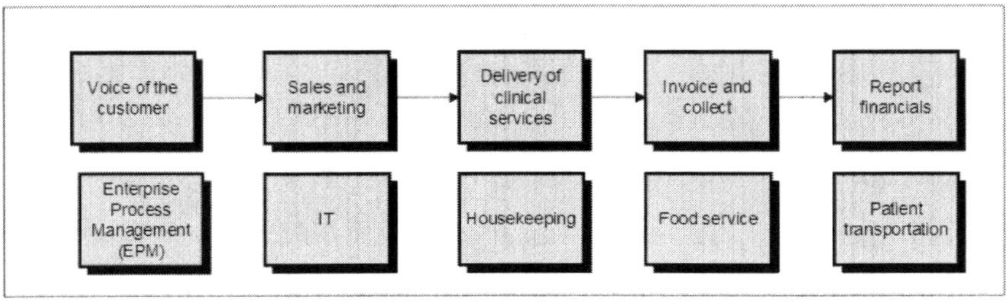

Figure 4.2: IEE value chain for a hospital

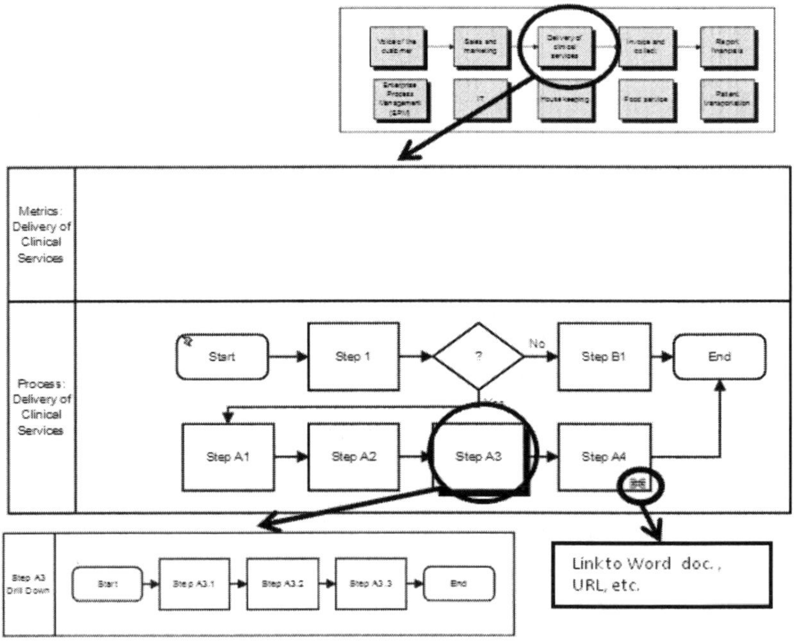

Figure 4.3: IEE value chain for a hospital highlighting process drill downs, where arrows describe IEE value chain drill downs.

The IEE value chain also structurally includes process performance measurements, as Figure 4.4 illustrates for the hospital example; hence, an IEE value chain basically describes what an organizational enterprise does, and how it measures what it does. The Enterprise Process Management (EPM) function in the figure could be created to manage the IEE BPM/EPM system.

Provided in an IEE value chain is a system for structurally documenting organizational processes with linkage to the resulting performance measurement output of these processes. In addition, IEE value chain performance measurements provide a predictive dashboard-reporting format that can have assigned ownership in an organization. This 30,000-foot-level reporting format has much benefit, including the reduction of organizational firefighting. The next chapter will provide more details on this topic.

Organizations benefit when up-to-date performance metric information is automatically updated so that all who have authority can access this information through a clickable interface. Enterprise Performance Reporting System (EPRS) software provides a means for creating this interface.

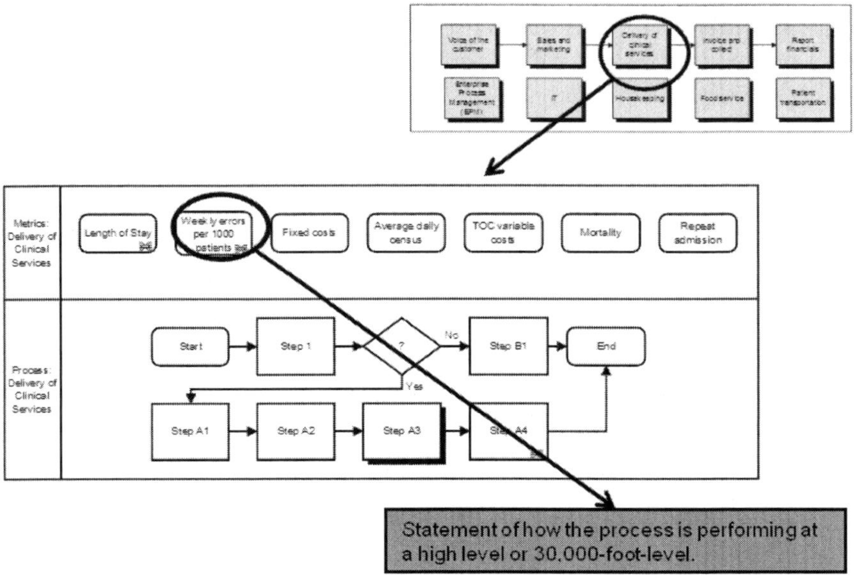

Figure 4.4: IEE value chain for a hospital highlighting a drill down to a 30,000-foot-level metric report, where arrows describe IEE value chain drill downs.

5

Process Management Performance Dashboards

You might ask why I am now discussing dashboards in this book since there is not much detailed discussion on this topic in other BPM and EPM literature. The reason is that process is the second word in both acronyms BPM and EPM. When we talk about processes, we should also include a discussion of how we are going to measure the effectiveness of these processes.

Organizational performance measures need to be reported in a BPM/EPM system so that the most beneficial behaviors occur; however, this action often does not occur with current reporting scorecard practices.

The following section will describe the issue with many current performance-reporting practices and what might be done differently to address this issue based on an assessment of the performance as common or uncommon.

5.1 Common-cause and Special-cause Variability

There are two categories that can separate the sources of variation or of change within any process.

- Common – variation and changes that are expected based on historical performance.
- Uncommon – changes that are not expected based on historical performance.

These categories provide a clear guidance on the follow-up actions to take if either of these conditions is unacceptable. Let's consider commuting time as an example to explain the differences.

Consider the time it takes for you to commute by car from home to work. Do we expect it to take the same amount of time every day, to the second? Obviously not; it will take longer some days than others because of traffic conditions, differing traveling speed one day from another, more delays on some days because of traffic signals, and so forth. These inputs to our commute-from-home-to-work process (*X*'s) would affect the output of the process (*Y*), the time it takes to commute in the relationship *Y=f(X),* where *f(X)* is a function of the *X's* or input values.

Let's consider that it typically takes between 25 and 35 minutes for you to commute. This *Y* variability would be considered the expected variation in time or as a common cause, the result from the expected variability of the inputs, *X*'s.

If it took you 60 minutes on a particular day, you could say that on this day there was a special cause, which we can talk about. Perhaps there was major inclement weather that day or there was a major traffic accident. However, you should not try to describe all the variability ups and downs of a common-cause variability condition. If you were to do this, much confusion could result, and there could be much wasted effort chasing common-cause variability as though it were special cause.

> *Background:*
>
> 30,000-foot-level is the IEE reporting of a process response which describes a high-level project or operation metric that

has infrequent subgrouping/sampling so that short-term variations, which might be caused by input random perturbations, will result in charts that view this variability as common cause.

Edwards Deming (Deming 1984) was the originator of the terms common cause and special cause. Statistical control charts are used to separate these two different types of variability, since the actions for these two types of conditions when occurring in a process can be quite different. Traditional control charts are used in manufacturing to identify when a special-cause condition occurs so that the process can be stopped for corrective action. This is not the objective of 30,000-foot-level measurement reporting, which gives focus to the determination of whether a process is stable and, if so, reporting how the process is performing relative to meeting the needs of the business.

Consider that you desired to reduce the amount of commute time from home to work. You might set a goal not to exceed 32 minutes for the commute. Over time you might be tracking your commute time, and if one day it took 33 minutes, you might try to understand why your goal was not met; however, if it took 31 minutes another day, you would not be taking any action since your goal was met.

However, we previously stated that this was not a good thing to do, since what would be occurring is that you would be reacting to common-cause variability as though it were special cause. This form of action can lead to much firefighting.

This illustration of goal setting is no different from the use of red-yellow-green scorecards in a business environment. With a stoplight scorecarding methodology, the red color appears whenever a goal is not being met at some point in time; e.g., 33 minutes in the previous illustration. Similarly a green signal would be reported whenever a measurement goal is being met; e.g., 31 minutes in the previous example.

The implications from the use of stoplight scorecarding in business processes are no different from what was illustrated in Deming's famous red bead experiment (Deming 1984). In his workshop's red-bead game, Deming had six "willing workers" from the audience use a paddle to randomly select 50 small beads from a large bowl, where 80 percent of the beads were white and 20 percent were red. A white bead symbolized a satisfactory occurrence, while a red bead indicated an unsatisfactory occurrence; hence, a draw of 15 beads from a worker could represent a non-conformance rate of 30 percent for that draw; i.e., 15 red beads from 50-holed paddle would be that 30 percent of the total beads selected were red.

When conducting this workshop experiment, Deming criticized workers who did not meet his goal of having no red beads. The number of red beads that an operator had in any particular paddle selection would actually be from the common-cause variability that one might suspect from drawing fifty beads from a population where 20% were red. Because of the high ratio of red to total beads in the bowl, it was almost impossible for a paddle draw to contain zero red beads.

What occurred during the red-bead workshop experiment was that whenever Deming either gave negative comments to a worker because he had increased the number of red beads from the last paddle draw or complemented another worker for reducing the number of red beads with a current paddle draw he was illustrating the impact of reacting to common-cause variability conditions as though they were special cause. What Deming illustrated as a business measurement problem in the 1980's is still occurring thirty years later!

When common-cause variability occurs in a process and the result is unsatisfactory, the process needs to be improved; i.e., in the above illustration, something must be done to reduce the proportion of red beads in the bowl. To understand what might be done to improve in a real-world process, hypotheses tests can be conducted with the intent of identifying process inputs that could be affecting the output of the process. With this understanding, changes might be made to the process inputs that later positively impacted the response of the process.

For our commute-from-home-to-work process, you might decide to see whether leaving one half-hour earlier, an input to our process, would reduce the time it takes for you to commute. Consider now that the results from this experiment indicated that your commute time is now between 18 and 22 minutes, a definite improvement from your original 25 to 35 minute commute times. Not only did your mean commute time reduce from this process change, but also the variability in commute time was less.

An IEE BPM/EPM system benefits when performance measures consider common-cause and special-cause variability in its reporting.

5.2 Reporting Performance

A scorecard helps manage an organization's performance through the optimization and alignment of organizational units, business processes, and individuals. A scorecard can also provide goals and targets, and helps individuals understand their organizational contribution.

Scorecards might span the operational, tactical, and strategic business aspects and decisions of any business. A dashboard displays information so that an enterprise can be run effectively. A dashboard organizes and presents information in a format that is easy to read and interpret.

These objectives are good; however, traditional scorecard practices using techniques such as stoplight scorecards, table of numbers, stacked bar charts, and pie charts have issues with achieving the stated desires. Frequently-used performance metrics and scorecard/dashboard reporting formats can create unhealthy, if not destructive, organizational behavior. (See *IEE Volume II*, Chapter 3 for more discussion on this topic.)

Traditional forms of measurement reporting often lead to stories about the past; however, what interests us the most is what we expect in the future, with the understanding that if what we expect to experience is undesirable, then something different needs to be done to change the course of the business' direction.

The enhancement business management system of IEE BPM/EPM with its 30,000-foot-level metric reporting system addresses the issues described above. In addition, 30,000-foot-level metrics provide a process predictive assessment, where, if a process has a recent region of stability, then the process can be stated to be predictable. When a prediction statement is made, data from the recent region of stability can be considered a random sample of the future in the formulation of this statement.

The steps for creating an IEE BPM/EPM scorecard/dashboard metric are:

1. Assess process predictability.
2. When the process is considered predictable, formulate a prediction statement for the latest region of stability. The usual reporting format for this statement is the following:
    a. When there is a specification requirement: nonconformance percentage or defects per million opportunities (DPMO).
    b. When there is no specification requirement: median response and 80 percent frequency of occurrence rate.

The IEE system can provide increased insight as to where improvement efforts would be most beneficial for the enterprise as a whole.

Summary

Organizations gain much when there is consistency in the reporting of performance measures across the organization. Much more is achieved when predictive performance reporting is provided with an alignment with the procedures that created the metrics, and these reports are periodically updated automatically with new process performance data. An approach for accomplishing this is described in the next chapter.

For further discussion about the formulation of IEE 30,000-foot-level metrics, see *IEE Volume III*, Chapters 12 and 13. For an illustration of the application of 30,000-foot-level metrics in an IEE value chain see *IEE Volume II*, Chapter 7.

6

Performance Management Through IEE Value Chain

With the Integrated Enterprise Excellence (IEE) approach, which integrates BPM and EPM, an IEE value chain is created so that there is alignment to the organization's vision and mission statements, as highlighted earlier in Figure 4.1.

With this IEE BPM/EPM form of reporting, if a performance measurement demonstrated common-cause variability and its performance level is not satisfactory, you would understand that the process would need to be improved in order to have a more desirable level of performance. In order to understand what might be done to improve the process, data from the process' recent region of stability can be helpful to test out various hypotheses to determine what might be done differently in the process. For example, if two people are making significantly more errors than others, perhaps the execution of a training process needs to be evaluated, in addition to targeted training for the two who are producing more non-conformances.

However, if a special-cause event occurs within the performance tracking of a process, then you might undertake a root-cause analysis to determine first what happened and secondly make corrective actions, if appropriate, with this causal analysis understanding.

Within the system that I am describing, this type of common-cause and special-cause analysis is part of management in executing both BPM and EPM.

Organizations benefit when the IEE value chain performance data are automatically updated (e.g., daily through an enterprise performance reporting system (EPRS) software) and presented in a clickable drill-down format where all who have authorization can access at any time the IEE value chain process information and aligned performance metrics. Since the core business of an organization typically remains constant over time, the IEE value chain is a long-lasting document that can be continually improved.

A company's organization chart provides the means to accomplish IEE value chain activities. With an IEE BPM/EPM approach to business-management, organizational changes do not structurally impact the IEE value chain; only process ownership and the performance of its metrics may be impacted by any reorganization that occur.

An IEE value chain should be created from a top-down perspective. An IEE value chain can incorporate and integrate an organization's primary/core processes, support processes, and management processes.

6.1 Enabling Technology That Automates Performance Reporting

Even if you create great process metrics and excellent process decision tools at the BPM level, this information must still be provided to the business management team though an EPM reporting structure. These process metrics need to be rolled up into an executive scorecard or equivalent that can be used to make high-level organizational and strategic decisions. This roll-up of metrics from the processes to the executive scorecard can be very labor intensive unless you plan for an automation of this task as part of your BPM deployment.

Many BPM software suites have a reporting function, but most are created for use by the process users for process control. The roll-up and creation of an executive scorecard is much different from what you would use for process management. Consider how:

- Metrics are often based on combining multiple process outputs.
- Measurement reporting should not be as focused on just today's performance but on the long term trends and the prediction of future performance expectations.
- Metrics should be assessing whether strategic plans are changing business performance across the organization.
- Measurements should be efficient at reporting the overall business performance to allow for better strategic planning and improvement opportunity identification.
- Metric reporting should be able to seamlessly handle data sources that exist throughout many different databases and files across the organization.

You have two choices: manually building these scorecards or implementing an automated reporting system to save you labor. One such system is the Smarter Solutions' Enterprise Performance Reporting System (EPRS). EPRS is a server-based solution that is able to provide automated performance reporting and scorecards, which allows for a performance metric report to be set up one time, and then a scheduling function will ensure that the reporting is kept up-to-date as the data sources change.

With this form of reporting, no additional labor is required to populate the executive scorecard, unless you recognize a change and want to update the reporting format or settings. All scorecard report access is achieved through a standard web browser. The EPRS system uses any existing network data sources to produce spectacular charts and capability assessments with little routine labor requirements.

6.2 EPM Routine Performance Reviews

With a system that provides a web-based IEE value chain and performance reports, which are automatically updated, anyone who is authorized can examine current procedures and their 30,000-foot-level performance statements.

At the business process management level, process owners and those involved in executing a process might evaluate their process performance measurements and procedures daily or weekly. The value chain could be used in the meeting to address common-cause variability issues and the status of process improvement efforts or simulations that could be executed with the purpose of improving a process' output.

At the enterprise process management level, reviews might be regularly conducted monthly or quarterly to assess the status of the metrics that are to be improved through the execution of projects, along with the status of completing these undertakings. The organization's Enterprise Improvement Plan (EIP) (discussed later in this book) might also be addressed to determine what other metrics might be undertaken for improvement with the overall objective of enhancing the bottom line.

Summary

Organizations can benefit much from an IEE value chain. For one thing, the IEE value chain provides a common platform for alignment of processes with their performance report-out, where this information could be readily accessed by all who have authorization.

The 30,000-foot-level predictive performance reporting methodology provides much benefit over traditional red-yellow-green scorecards, pie charts, stacked bar charts, and table of numbers, all of which are not unlike driving a car by only looking at the rear view window, an unhealthy practice.

What organizations need is a system that looks out the windshield, where, if what is seen is not desirable, the brakes need to be applied or the steering wheel turned, not unlike execution of a process improvement effort. The 30,000-foot-level reporting system provides a means to accomplish this objective.

For further discussion about this IEE value chain topic, see *IEE Volume II*, Chapter 7 and *IEE Volume III*, Chapters 12 and 13.

7

Establishing a Solid EPM System in a BPM/EPM Deployment

Enterprise Process Management (EPM) is an aspect of a BPM deployment that was earlier shown graphically in Figure 2.1. EPM within an IEE BPM/EPM deployment is highlighted in Figure 7.1. Example tools that could be applied when executing this system are highlighted in the middle of the figure using an oblong shape. More specifically, the steps of EPM in an IEE implementation, with the inclusion of the first two steps previously described (i.e., vision/mission and IEE value chain), are shown in Figure 7.2.

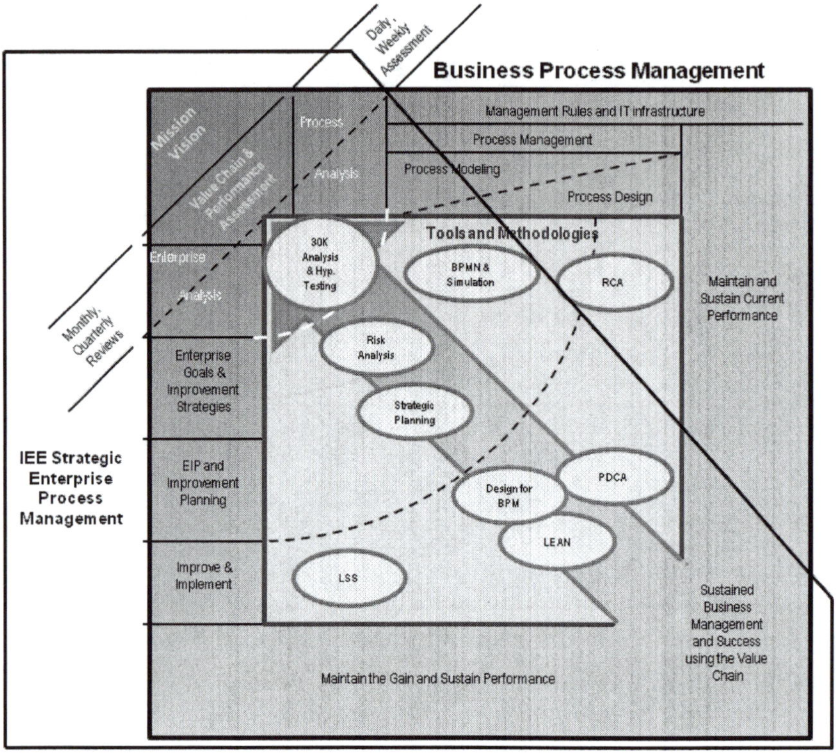

Figure 7.1: Highlighting EPM in the IEE BPM/EPM roadmap.

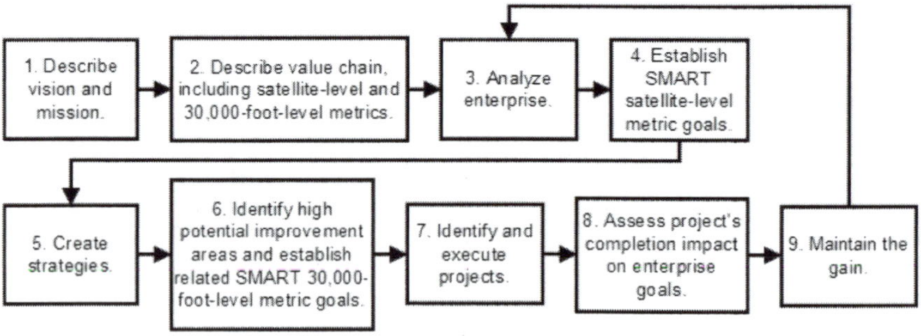

Figure 7.2: IEE EPM 9-step system.

7.1 EPM Implementation Steps

The following describes the basic thought process of executing the EPM steps described in Figure 7.2.

- Step 1
  - Define vision and mission.
- Step 2
  - Describe value chain, including 30,000-foot-level metrics.
  - Create satellite-level metrics for the past three to ten years. We want to ensure that the selected time is long enough that multiple business cycles are captured.
  - Compile 30,000-foot-level value chain metrics.
- Step 3
  - Analyze satellite-level and 30,000-foot-level metrics looking for improvement opportunities.
  - Analyze the enterprise as a whole looking for constraints, improvement opportunities, and new product opportunities, which could include acquisitions or selling portions of the business.
- Step 4
  - Establish specific, measurable, actionable, relevant, and time-based (SMART) goals that are consistent with the work from step 3.
- Step 5
  - Create strategies from step analyses described in step three.
- Step 6
  - Identify high potential areas and related 30,000-foot-level scorecard/dashboard metrics for focusing

improvement efforts using goals and the value-chain process map to help guide the selection process.

  - Establish 30,000-foot-level value chain metric goals with agree-to ownership and time for achievement. The project champion should be the owner of the metric that is to be improved.
  - Identify potential projects that are in alignment with determined business needs.

- Step 7
  - Select and assign well-scoped projects that are not too large or too small.
  - Work for timely project completion of process using resource of champion and black belt or green belt with coaching.
- Step 8
  - Assess project completion impact on enterprise goals.
- Step 9
  - Maintain the gains
  - Repeat.

To reiterate, IEE 30,000-foot-level performance metrics are high-level operational metrics. This form of metric reporting can also provide the baseline that improvement projects are to enhance.

The right metrics are needed for the orchestration of the right activities. The EPM process just described accomplishes this by linking improvement activities to business goals and to strategies that are aligned with these goals through the use of analytics.

You can also use this strategy with other types of improvement efforts for objectives such as reliability excellence and behavior-based safety. People in organizations often feel overwhelmed when facing multiple improvement activities and when resources are in competition between associated projects. This system can tie all the improvement practices together and prioritize resource utilization so that efforts are spent where there is the most need. This high-level approach for determining where to target resources can help organizations understand and improve the key drivers that affect the metrics and enterprise process scorecards.

For further discussion about this IEE implementation of EPM, see *IEE Volume II.*

8

EPM: Analyze the Enterprise

To be successful, organizations need to make high-level business decisions. These decisions can be made through instincts and/or data analyses. People can be very successful leading a company by relying heavily on their instincts using minimal data analyses. However, often what might be thought as the best approach or strategy may be found not to be so when data are analyzed. Or, if the lead person for historically making beneficial instinct-based decisions is no longer available (such as in the Steve Jobs example cited at the beginning of this book), the enterprise can quickly lose its way.

In the IEE system, the EPM analyze phase, as highlighted in Figures 8.1 and 8.2, does not suggest that the use of instincts is bad and should be avoided. Instead, effort should be given to create a system that efficiently and effectively combines structural data with instincts and organizational wisdom. In this system, data analyses can later provide insight to which decisions were beneficial and which ones were not. Through these analyses, a learning organization can develop which knows what could be done differently the next time to create better results. The overall goal of this integration is to create a Results Orchestration (RO) system that moves toward achieving the three Rs of business; i.e., everyone doing the right things and doing them right at the right time.

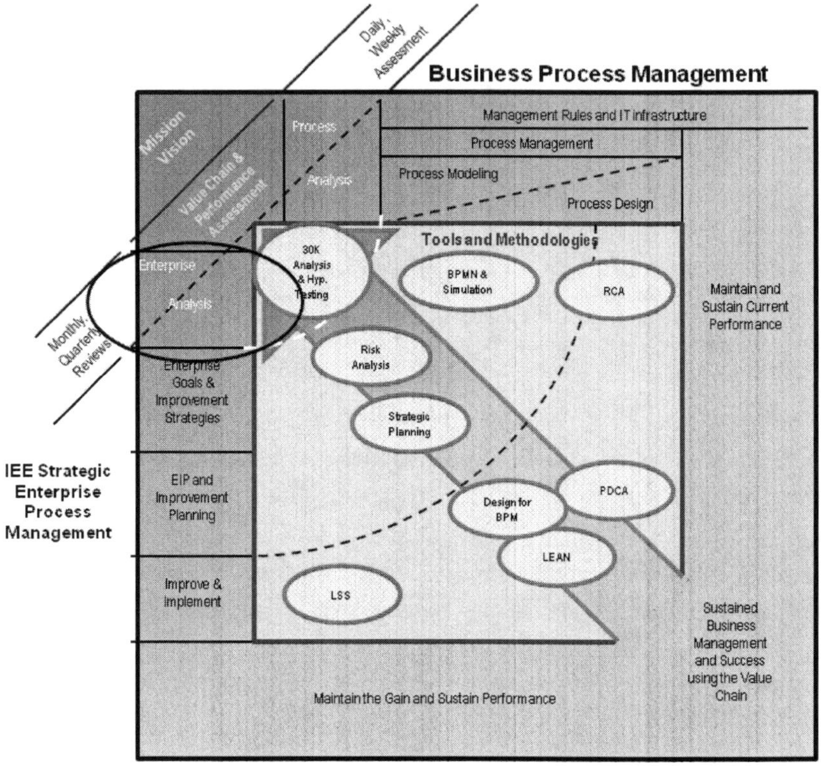

Figure 8.1: Highlighting EPM analysis in the IEE BPM/EPM roadmap.

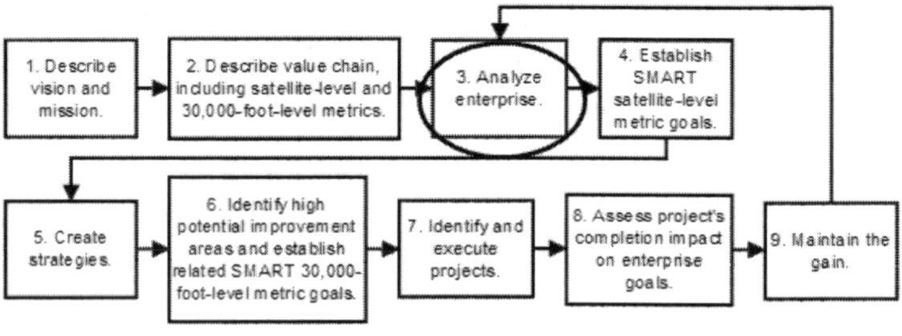

Figure 8.2: Highlighting analysis in the IEE EPM system.

For most organizations, many business analysis systems already exist. Often these systems are ad hoc, dependent upon a particular person to execute the process, or have a large opportunity for improvement. In the IEE EPM analyze phase, there is a focus for system identification, coordination, and improvement.

8.1 Whole-system Analysis for Improving the Financials

Many items should be structurally considered when conducting a whole-system analysis for the purpose of improving a business. A list of items that should be considered is provided later in this chapter.

In the effort to determine where improvement efforts should focus, much insight can be gained through an examination of the IEE value chain, which can lead to the creation of projects that address:

- Rules/policy change needs
- Operational metric improvement needs that have whole-system benefits; e.g., reducing defective rates which have large negative impact on corporate profits or reducing operational waste to improved operational delivery response time
- New market opportunities
- Process automation opportunities

Organizations may conduct a SWOT analysis in strategic planning to determine their strengths, weaknesses, opportunities, and threats. This information can be useful when integrated with the other techniques described in the analyze phase of the EPM roadmap; however, SWOT inputs need to incorporate a good blend of data decision-making with intuition. A clear, long-lasting mechanism for project selection is needed so that the business as a whole benefits and silo-only-benefited or individual-pet projects are avoided.

8.1.1 *Potential Projects: Rules/Policy Projects*

I can remember having a conversation with a Lean Six Sigma deployment lead of an 80-billion-dollar company who was boasting about how his company had been saving 30 million dollars annually for many years. I stated that this amount of savings was impressive; however, I wondered how much benefit his CEO was actually seeing, since 30 million dollars in savings is relatively small when compared to 80 billion dollars in revenue.

Some of the most significant gains can be made through making changes in the rules or policies within a company, which traditional process improvement programs don't address. An example of an improvement effort with this line of thinking might address an organization's compensation system. The question you might ask yourself is: Does this compensation really benefit the enterprise financials as a whole? To illustrate this point, consider:

- Does it make sense to compensate the sales force with a bonus if they meet their total quarterly revenue goals (which were arbitrarily set) when a data analysis shows that most sales occur during the last few weeks of each quarter because of the sales force's offering customers special deals that lead to less corporate profit and additional frustration and overtime in manufacturing to deliver the products in a timely fashion? Should the sales-force commission policy be changed to address this issue?
- Does it make sense to provide bonuses throughout an organization against arbitrary quarterly goals when the company is losing money? Might it be better to incorporate a corporate profit-sharing plan, since this compensation approach could lead to less playing games with the numbers and increased focus on cross-functional teams working together for enterprise-as-a-whole benefits?

Another rule or policy illustration that might be challenged is: does it make sense to select suppliers who provide the lowest costs when our experience is that often these suppliers have the poorest quality, which leads to additional business cost, much frustration, and potential customer loss because of dissatisfaction from product quality issues? Should this vendor selection process rule/policy be improved?

The IEE EPM system provides a structure for addressing this need for creating or adjusting rules/policies so that the enterprise as a whole benefits.

8.1.2 *Potential Projects: Operational Performance Measurement Improvement*

Organizations typically select improvement projects from a list of potential projects that people believe are important to provide some financial savings. Often the decisions for these improvement efforts are opinion-based and not selected from evaluating the enterprise as a whole. The result of this traditional selection process for improvement projects is that resulting project definition:

- May address silo issues but have little impact on the enterprise as a whole since the overall business constraint was not addressed.
- May lead to a Lean kaizen event that resulted in everyone feeling good; however, there was no graphical description or statistical analysis showing how the change impacted any organizational performance metric.
- Is not aligned and tracked against improving a performance metric. Because of this lack of alignment to scorecard and dashboard metrics, process owners are not often compelled to actively support a process improvement efforts in their areas since the alignment of the project to what they are getting measured against is not apparent. The implication of this is that many process improvement projects never get completed.

To illustrate the ineffectiveness of many process improvement efforts, consider the following, which is not unlike what happens in many deployments:

> At a major defense contractor conference, where I was conducting a keynote presentation, the General Manager gave a presentation stating how the company had seen much benefit from Lean. In a tour of the GM's facility, I commented on how much benefit was apparent from their Lean effort. I then stated how it was apparent that their machines were underutilized. I then asked about the improvement projects that they were undertaking in sales and marketing. I only received a blank stare. They were doing nothing to address the obvious organizational constraint for improving their financials; i.e., sales and marketing.

A methodology is needed where enterprise-wide measurement improvement needs "pull" for projects to enhance key performance indicators (KPIs) that benefit the business as a whole, and the owners of these metrics are asking for timely project completions; e.g., to reduce the costs of doing nothing differently (DODND) in a process through executing a root-cause analysis.

The IEE EPM system provides a structure for addressing this need for selecting and executing projects that positively impact performance metrics that benefit the enterprise as a whole.

8.1.3 *Potential Projects: New Market Opportunities*

Steve Jobs, the late co-founder, chairman, and CEO of Apple Inc., superbly orchestrated the selection of new opportunities for his company. However, not every organization has a person like Steve Jobs leading its business.

Often executive decisions, such as entering a new market (or building a new facility or closing an existing facility), are based on intuition of a few people without structurally or statistically evaluating data and related risks.

Organizations benefit when there is a structured decision-making mechanism at the executive level that includes inputs from all levels of the organization.

The IEE EPM system provides the structure for selecting new markets and opportunities that positively impact the enterprise as a whole.

8.1.4 *Potential Projects: Process Automation Opportunities*

An organization might undertake a BPM initiative where the primary motivation is to automate their processes. But is this the best approach for implementing BPM? To address this question, consider that:

- Process automation can be beneficial; however, not all processes need to be automated.
- It is important to have a system for improving a process before its automation; otherwise, an organization can more efficiently create an unsatisfactory transaction.
- The selection of which processes to automate can lead to organizational silo benefits that do not have much positive impact on the enterprise as a whole.
- The selection of which process to automate should have a structural integration with the organization's dashboard/scorecarding system.

The IEE EPM system provides the structure for selecting which processes should be automated so that the enterprise as a whole benefits. Characteristics of processes where automation can have the most benefit are processes that have:

- High variability
- Much dependency upon an individual
- Customer interaction
- Too much labor
- Cost too much
- Unsatisfactorily slow performance

8.2 EPM Analyze Phase

In the IEE EPM analyze phase, focus is given to the satellite and enterprise level performance metrics. Each key metric is evaluated over time and in comparison to the performance expectation. When a performance is found not to meet expectation, then a deeper analysis is performed.

An underperforming enterprise metric analysis involves an assessment of the processes that provide the performance and their process inputs. Many common tools are used such as Pareto charts, control charts, comparison testing, and more. In many cases, the analysis will drill down to a process to include the people operating the process and the source of the material or transaction. The analysis is not an improvement effort, but more of a root-cause analysis.

IEE Volume II, Chapter 8 provides a checklist guide to determine where you might concentrate your efforts to gain this insight.

9

EPM: Establishing Goals, Creating Strategies, and Identification of Improvement Projects

Dr. Lloyd S. Nelson (Deming 1986) stated: "If you can improve productivity, or sales, or quality, or anything else, by (e.g.,) five percent next year without a rational plan for improvement, then why were you not doing it last year?"

When organizations establish scorecard goals, much care needs to be exercised. Goals should be SMART. However, these guidelines are often violated. Arbitrary goals set for individuals or organizations can be very counterproductive and costly.

The implication of Nelson's statement is that simple goal setting alone will not yield an improved output. For an improved output, organizations need to give due diligence to bettering the process. This volume focuses on the creation of more customers and cash, not the simple creation of arbitrary goals throughout the organization, which can lead to the wrong activities or strategies that often result in interpretation and action-item inconsistencies.

The establishment of goals, creation of strategies, and identification of improvement projects fit into the overall IEE implementation of EPM as shown in Figures 9.1 and 9.2, which will be discussed in this chapter.

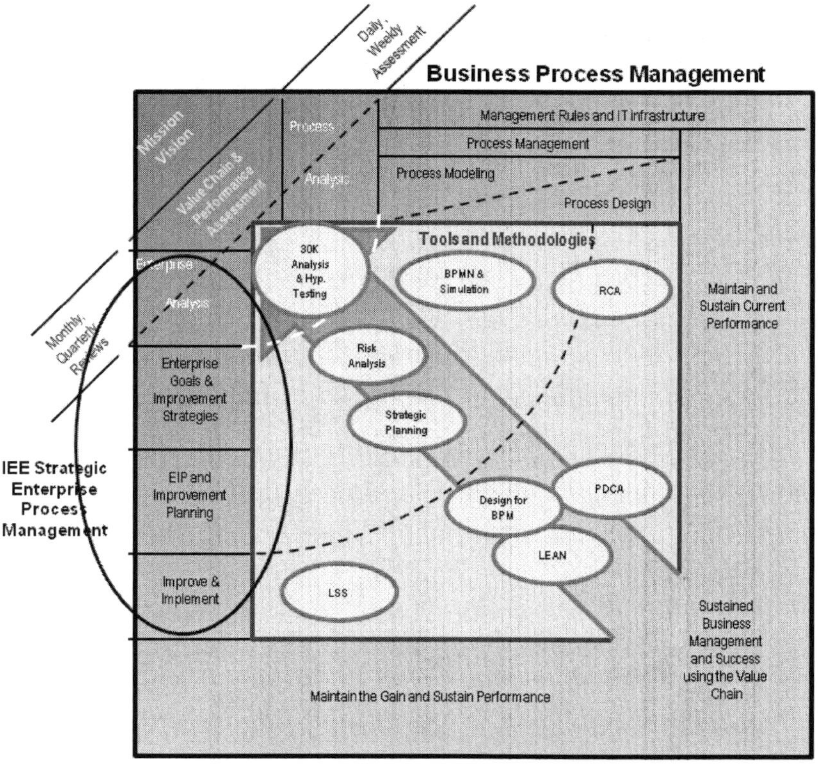

Figure 9.1: Highlighting aspects of the IEE BPM/EPM roadmap.

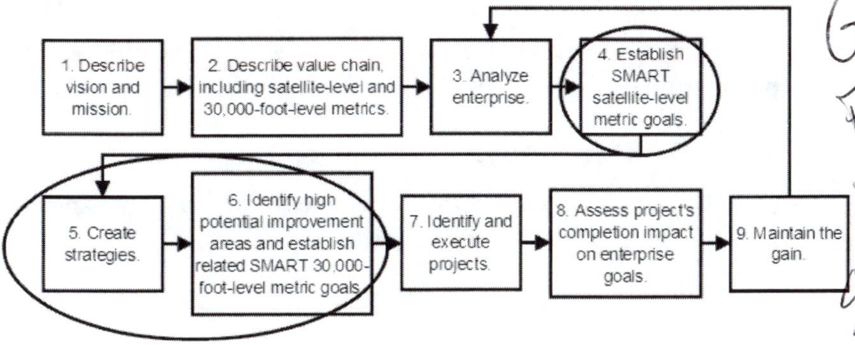

Figure 9.2: Highlighting aspects of the IEE EPM system.

9.1 Establishing Financial and Operational Goals

In the IEE implementation of EPM, satellite-level and 30,000-foot-level dashboard metrics are examined over time before financial goals are established. The assessment of these non-calendar-bounded metrics helps with the creation of SMART goals. This assessment could lead to the following mean monthly satellite-level metric goals:

- Sales growth: 10 percent
- Operating margins: 20 percent
- ROCE (return on capital employed): 20 percent

Other organizational goals that could be tracked at the 30,000-foot-level dashboard metric level are the following:

- Environmental: Energy cost reductions of at least 25 percent over three years.
- New products: 30 percent of products sold have been available five years or less.

Satellite-level enterprise-process goals can be drilled down to 30,000-foot-level goals and then to specific projects that facilitate the process of achieving these goals, which will be described later in this volume.

9.2 Creating Strategies

Strategic thinking is important to the business. A strategic analysis includes (Hambrick and Fredrickson 2001) the following:

- Industrial analysis
- Customer or marketplace trends
- Environmental forecast
- Competitor analysis
- Assessment of internal strengths, weakness, resources

Organizations often build strategies around statements like "develop strategic relationship with industry leaders." How does an organization interpret and measure success against such a statement like this? What makes matters worse is that these strategies are then cascaded throughout the whole organization, and functional goals are set against them. Could there be different interpretations for these strategies? Of course there could be. What happens when leadership changes? Do the strategies change? I would again say yes, and the change could lead to havoc with a redo of many organizational metrics.

A strategy needs to be dynamic so that it can address timely changes and flexible so that it can address multiple options. It needs to be able to form an effective assessment of current conditions for the creation of a meaningful two – three year plan. Most strategic plans emphasize only one or two components of what is truly needed.

IEE Volume II, Figure 8.1 provides five elements of a strategic development process.

9.3 Identification of Focus Areas for Improving the Financials

As part of EMP, executives want to improve the financials; however, where should these efforts focus? This is what I would like to address in this section.

A team can compile and present this information in an enterprise improvement plan (EIP) format, as illustrated in Figure 9.3. In this figure, steps of the 9-step EPM process are noted within the associated columns.

Whenever possible, it is most desirable if the high potential area reflects a value-chain metric that has management ownership and specific objectives. High potential area targets need to be determined using financial and other analyses, including the current IEE value chain performance. From this effort, end-to-end processes that need to improve can be identified and undertaken as an improvement project.

9.4 Building an Enterprise Improvement Plan (EIP)

Enterprise improvements listed in an EIP can take many forms. Identified organizational improvements can be the automation of a process, a change in organizational rules/policies, another company merger, or a process improvement undertaking. A selection of one or more of these efforts is targeted specifically to benefit the enterprise's big picture.

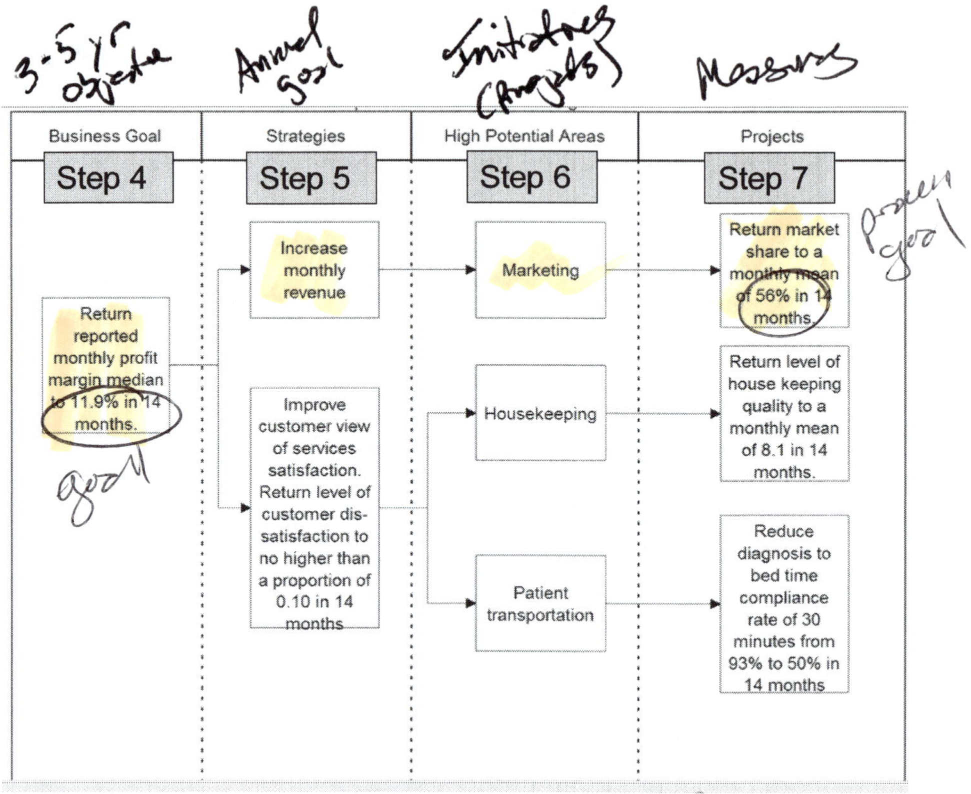

Figure 9.3: Enterprise Improvement Plan (EIP) where highlighted numbers indicate steps of the 9-step system shown in Figure 9.2.

The Enterprise Process Management (EPM) function (e.g., as illustrated in Figure 4.2) could own the EIP execution. The following illustrates how a technical team can work with executive management to generate an EIP formulation.

- Compile and present the value chain and its metrics to executives.
- Work with executives to create SMART goals for the satellite-level metrics.

- Conduct an EPM analysis, working with various teams such as customer representatives, to develop various strategies that could be undertaken to meet these objectives.
- Summarize EPM analyses to executives and work with them to define EIP strategies.
- Work with teams to define EIP high potential areas and then drill down to project opportunities.
- Assign an owner to each selected project. If a value-chain metric is to be improved through the completion of a project, then the process owner would be responsible for the metric's improvement through the satisfactory completion of the project.

Summary

Organizations need a system for improving operations and determining what should be done differently in the business to improve their financials. Improving customer satisfaction and improving efficiencies, among other items, are important; however, often these efforts are undertaken in silos and don't positively impact the big picture; e.g., we saved 100 million dollars, but nobody can find the money.

A systematic approach is needed within EPM for addressing these needs and orchestrating not only process improvement projects but also generation/modification of rules and policies. For this to occur, evaluation needs to begin at the enterprise as a whole and work downward, which the IEE EPM system provides.

10

EPM: How to Improve the Business As a Whole

Executives make decisions on what could be done differently to improve the business as a whole. Each of these efforts can be viewed as a project. The selection and execution of efforts fit into the overall IEE implementation of EPM as shown in Figures 10.1 and 10.2. This topic will now be discussed in this chapter.

Previously it was described how business improvement efforts should be targeted so that the enterprise as a whole benefits. Four areas for improvement considerations are:

- Rules/policy change needs
- Operational metric improvement needs that have whole-system benefits
- New market opportunities
- Process automation opportunities

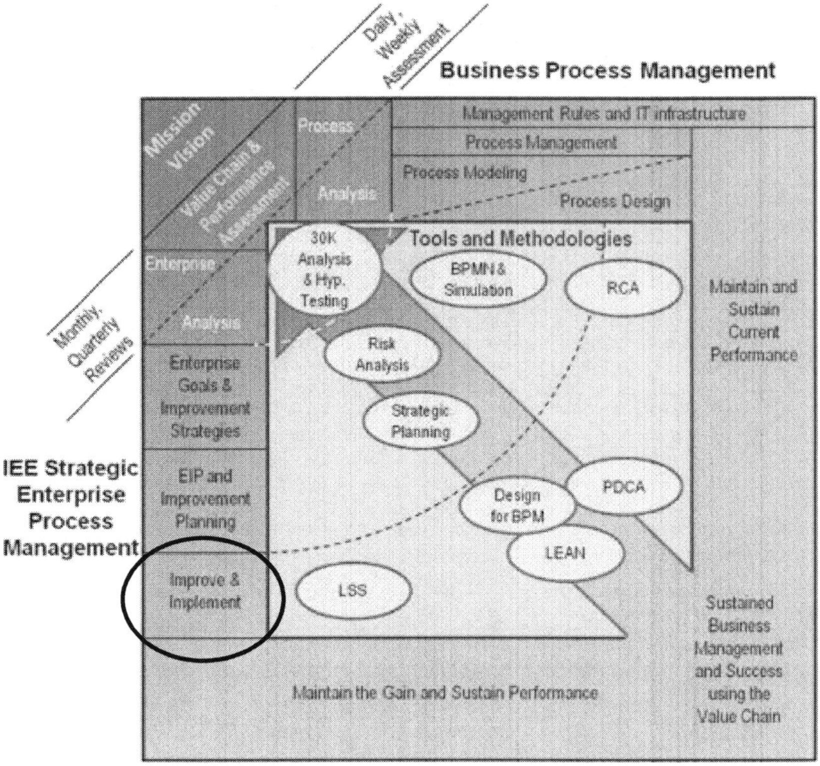

Figure 10.1: Highlighting an aspect of the IEE BPM/EPM roadmap.

It is important to realize that all improvement opportunities are not handled as a Lean Six Sigma or other big project effort. Some improvement opportunities may be to research a topic or to test a market, or to just go do something.

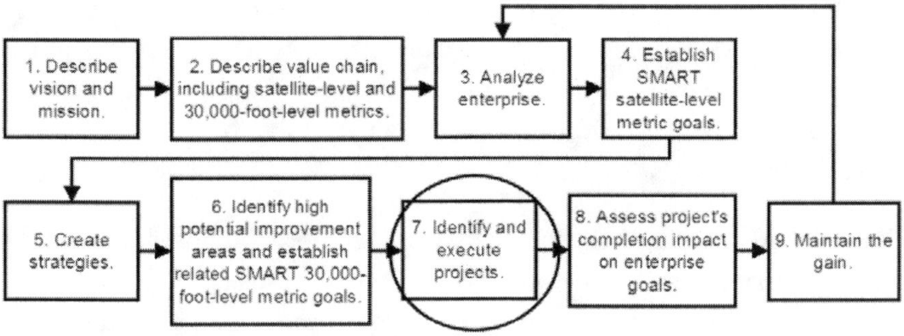

Figure 10.2: Highlighting an aspect of the IEE EPM system.

10.1 Selecting an Improvement Approach

To undertake improvement project execution, one of the following methodologies can be undertaken (See *IEE Volume III* for application of the tools below):

- Special-cause condition (solution known)
    - Just do it
- Special cause condition (solution unknown)
    - Root-cause analysis, fault tree analysis
- Common-cause condition (solution known)
    - Lean project: 5S, kaizen, value stream map (VSM), low hanging fruit
- Common-cause condition (solution unknown)
    - Plan-Do-Check-Act (PDCA): Continuous improvement
    - Lean Six Sigma Define-Measure-Analyze-Improve-Control (DMAIC) process improvement roadmap or design for Six Sigma roadmap

All improvements may not have an associated metric; however, whenever possible, efforts to improve the business should have a before-process-change 30,000-foot-level metric that is to transition to an enhanced level of performance after an effective process change has been implemented.

This 30,000-foot-level metric that is to be improved should be within the organization's IEE value chain, where the process owner is assigned the task for improving the process that impacts that metric; hence, this process owner is actively asking the process improvement practitioners how they are progressing relative to completing the project management activities associated with the project (See *IEE Volume III* checklist for project completion, Tables E.1 – E.9).

10.2 Common Cause Condition (Solution Unknown)

I thought it would be beneficial to elaborate on the execution of one type of improvement project and its relation to analyses; i.e., common-cause condition where the solution is unknown.

For this situation, you can view the 30,000-foot-level metric (i.e., Y in the relationship $Y=f(x)$) to determine at what point in time the process reached its current level of performance. A brainstorming session could then be executed with the intent of uncovering X's that could be affecting process performance. For example, if defect rate is being tracked over time, a Pareto chart might indicate that a particular type of transaction is causing the most defective units. Another example is a project that is to reduce lead time might uncover using a dot plot and analysis of means (ANOM) that a particular operation is causing the most amount of delay in providing timely order completion.

10.3 Reporting the Progress of Improvement Projects

A process owner may be responsible to report-out monthly to executive management the status of how the performance metric improvement need is progressing relative to the completion of the project. Note how this is different from many process improvement project efforts where focus is giving to quantification of the financial benefits or projects;

i.e., a push for project creation that is not aligned to the business management system. Organizations can gain more and have more timely completion of projects if overall organization metric improvement needs pull for timely project completion.

11

EPM: Maintaining the Gain and Sustaining Performance

Maintaining the gain and sustaining performance fit into the overall IEE implementation of EPM as shown in Figures 11.1 and 11.2, which will be discussed in this chapter.

In the IEE system, how an improvement positively impacts the business as a whole was described in the organization's EIP, as illustrated in Figure 9.3. Upon completion of an improvement, you should assess how well the effort's completion fulfilled its initial objectives.

If care is not taken, a process can revert back to its previous ways of execution, stalling out the gains that the improvement effort provided. Some improvement effort executions require the use of control measures so that the resulting process performance is maintained.

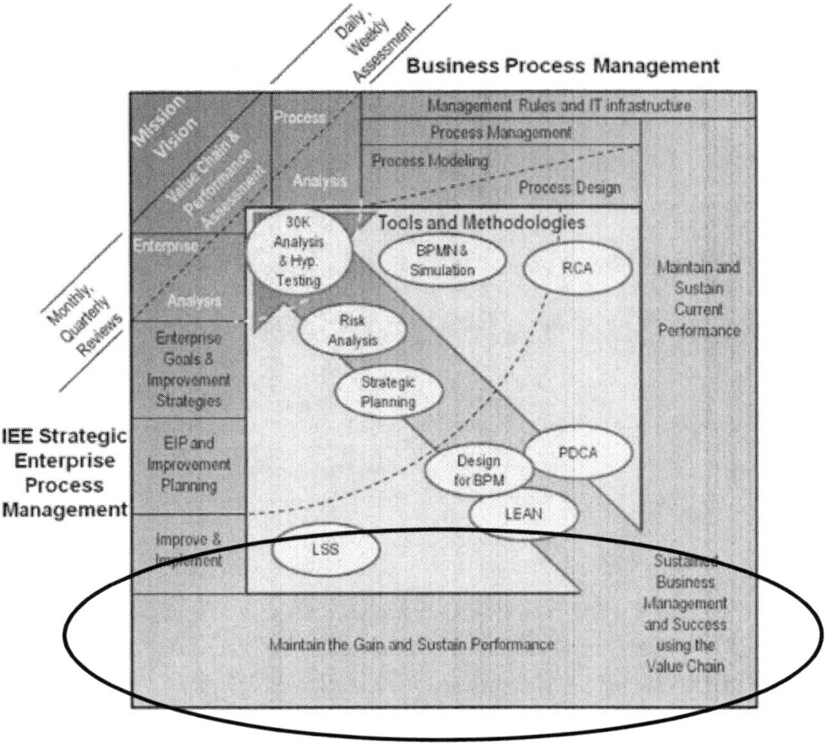

Figure 11.1: Highlighting an aspect of the IEE BPM/EPM roadmap.

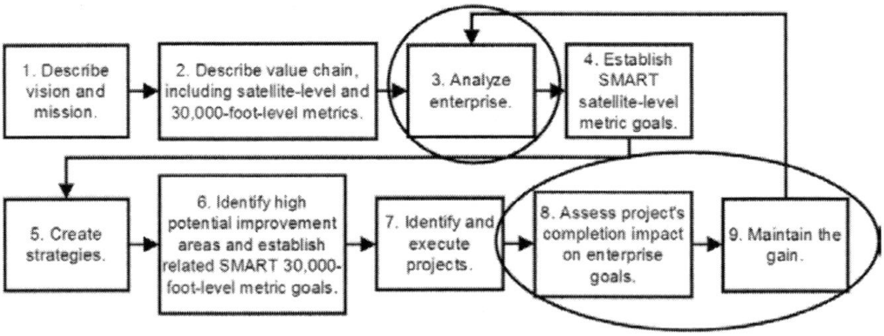

Figure 11.2: Ensure processes stay aligned to strategic needs and adjust to improvement needs.

The effectiveness of these controls and the tracking of their performance can be monitored through an Enterprise Performance Reporting System (EPRS), which automatically updates IEE value chain reported metrics periodically (e.g., daily) for all to see through a simple click. In addition, the overall process performance can be tracked through the IEE value chain, where the process owner has responsibility for maintaining the gain.

IEE process performance tracking through the value chain can identify for the process owner the occurrence of special-cause conditions that need timely resolution; i.e., maintaining the gain. Through this control mechanism, we can also ensure that BPM rules are being executed appropriately and that our processes stay aligned and are adjusted appropriately to meet an organization's overall business needs.

12

BPM in a BPM/EPM Deployment and Process Management

In previous chapters, focus was given to the aspects of EPM in a BPM/EPM deployment. Focus will now change toward implementing BPM as part of a BPM/EPM deployment using the Integrated Enterprise Excellence (IEE) system roadmap, as shown in Figure 12.1. Example tools that could be applied when executing this system are highlighted in the middle of the figure using an oblong shape.

As the name suggests, EPM provides direction on what could be done differently through examination of the enterprise as a whole in order to have good, long-lasting financials. This viewpoint downplays doing what it takes to meet the quarterly goals, which are often set arbitrarily without attention to what might need to be done differently at the process level to meet these goals. Instead a system was presented for what should be done to better meet/exceed customer needs/desires so that realistic long-lasting financial performance is achieved.

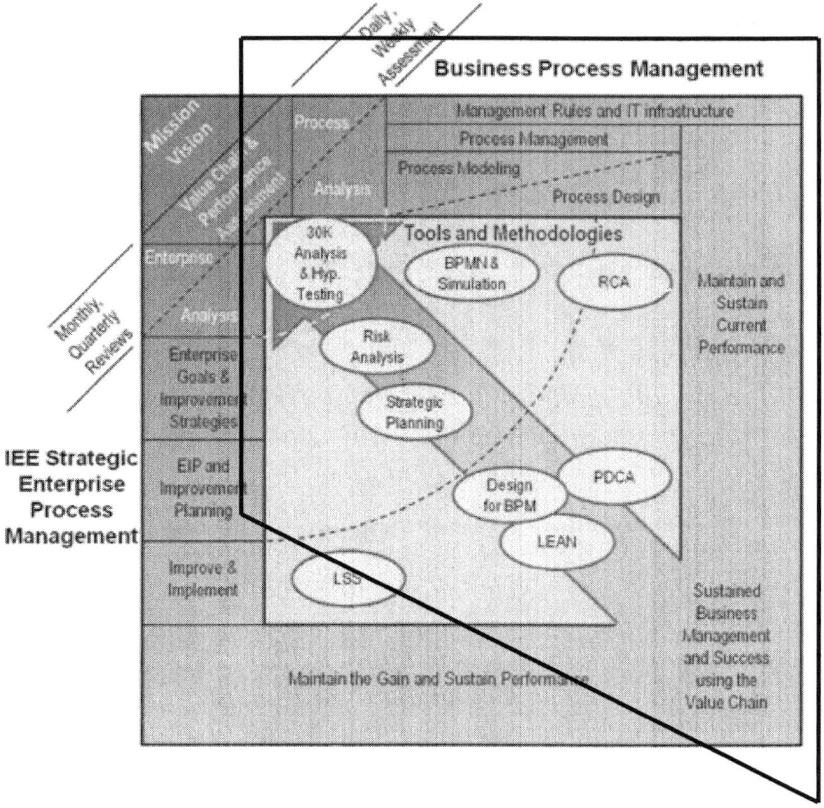

Figure 12.1: Highlighting BPM in the IEE BPM/EPM roadmap.

The *ABPMP BPM CBOK®* describes BPM as a "disciplined approach to identify, design, execute, document, measure, monitor, and control both automated and non-automated business processes to achieve consistent, targeted results aligned with an organization's strategic goals."

This portion of the book will provide a structure for addressing BPM implementation needs at the functional and process owner's level for addressing the core concepts listed in the *ABPMP BPM CBOK®*, which are:

- "BPM is a management discipline and a set of enabling technologies.
- BPM addresses end-to-end work and distinguishes between sets of sub-processes, tasks, activities, and functions.
- BPM is a continuous, ongoing set of processes focused on managing an organization's end-to-end business processes
- BPM includes the modeling, analysis, design, and measurement of an organization's business processes.
- BPM requires a significant organizational commitment, often introducing new roles, responsibilities, and structures to traditional functionally-oriented organizations.
- BPM is technology enabled with tools for visual modeling, simulation, automation, integration, control and monitoring of business processes and the information systems which support these processes."

12.1 Managing Organization's Business Processes

The previously described IEE value chain (see Chapter 6) provides the basis from which many of the listed *ABPMP BPM CBOK®* core concepts are addressed. How the IEE value chain directly addresses the first three core concepts:

- The IEE value chain provides a structure from which BPM can become a management discipline. The enterprise performance reporting system (EPRS) software provides an enabling technology that provides linkage of processes with performance reporting, which assesses process stability and how the process is performing relative to consistently meeting the needs of the business.

- The IEE value chain BPM provides a central repository for the documentation of end-to-end work and distinguishes between sets of sub-processes, tasks, activities, and functions.
- The IEE value chain provides means for establishing a continuous, ongoing set of processes focused on managing an organization's end-to-end business processes.

Other core components of a BPM initiative will be discussed in future chapters.

The *ABPMP BPM CBOK®* notes how confusion often exists between business process management (BPM) and business process improvement (BPI) initiatives. BPI gives focus to one-time projects which provide unique improvements to fix a process, while BPM implies a permanent, ongoing organizational commitment to managing the organization's processes. The EPRS software provides the enabling technology for displaying up-to-date IEE value chain process descriptions and performance measures, which are readily available to everyone throughout the world who has access authorization.

12.2 BPM Lifecycle

ABPMP BPM CBOK® summarizes the BPM lifecycle as an iterative set of activities that include: planning; analysis; design and modeling; implementation; monitoring and control; refinement. When businesses move through this lifecycle, they are enabled or constrained by factors which include leadership, values, culture, and beliefs.

An objective of this book's described BPM/EPM model is to provide a systematic approach for leadership to orchestrate the implementation of BPM so that in addition to the business gaining much, there is consistency in maintaining its values, culture, and beliefs.

Although the following chapters reference BPM in their titles, the described techniques can be used at both the business process management level as well as the EPM level.

12.3 Achievement of BPM Critical Success Factors

In Section 2.1 of this book, the following *BPM CBOK®* book listing of four BPM critical success factors were presented. I have now added to each of these items a description how the IEE BPM/EPM implementation addresses each success factor:

1. Define corporate-wide business process value chains and leadership: The IEE value chain provides the structure for making the company's core business activities. The EPRS software provides the enabling technology for disseminating this information. In the IEE value chain, process and performance metric ownership is assigned.
2. Measure process chain performance: The IEE value chain provides the structure for the management of scorecards/dashboards with accountability. The EPRS software provides the enabling technology for disseminating this information.
3. Institutionalize practices: The IEE BPM/EPM system that has been described in this book provides a system for incorporating continuous improvement, management of process governance, enabling change management, and the leveraging of BPM products.
4. Standardize business processes: The IEE value chain provides a vehicle for adoption of common design/engineering methodology, documentation of processes, and management of process diversity.

13

BPM: Process Analysis

One critical success factor of BPM is the establishment of enterprise and business unit goals to meet the business' strategy. In the previously described EPM process, the enterprise as a whole was analyzed to establish business financial goals and targeted strategies that lead to process goals that positively impact the big picture. Each of the process owners was then responsible for working with a team that was to determine what should be done differently in the process in order to achieve their goal.

With this approach for enterprise as a whole improvement, it is understood that all processes do not need to be improved in order for the business to have good financials that do not sacrifice long-term organizational health and also provide excellent customer satisfaction.

An EPM analysis approach gives emphasis to targeting the bottleneck/constraint, and/or rules/policies of the organization as a whole to make improvements. Organizational end-to-end processes that are thought important from this assessment are to be the focus of these improvement efforts, which could involve process automation. In addition to this constraint-assessment effort, an overall EPM assessment could also lead to other big-picture beneficial work such as an innovative undertaking, an expansion/contraction of the business, and/or goals being established to improve additional business processes; e.g., a reduction of defective rates that are negatively impacting profit margins.

Let's now consider BPM analysis activity, as shown in Figure 12.1. BPM analyses could be executed by process owners or analysts throughout in the organization at the same time as an EPM analysis. In this analysis, the 30,000-foot-level metrics for a process, as a drill down of the IEE value chain, should first be assessed for stability. If the process is stable, then hypothesis tests could be undertaken to determine what might be done to improve the process. The logic, in general, for improving an individual process would be similar to what was described for the enterprise in the previous EPM discussion (See Sections 10.1 and 10.2).

13.1 Analyses to Improvement

From this analysis or assessment of every process prior to applying the BPM concepts, an organization should consider an improvement or standardization effort to ensure that the new process is optimal for the organizational needs. The activities that could result from an analysis to improve an IEE value chain 30,000-foot-level metric include:

- A Lean kaizen event might be undertaken since it was thought that this would improve the process workflow and its resulting performance metric.
- A Lean Six Sigma project could be undertaken following a DMAIC project execution roadmap.
- The process might be modeled for improved work flow or optimization.
- The process might be redesigned.
- The process might be automated.

For more detailed information about process analyses see:

- 30,000-foot-level metrics: *IEE Volume III*, Chapters 12 and 13

- Hypothesis testing: *IEE Volume III*, Chapters 19 – 28
- Lean Six Sigma DMAIC roadmap: *IEE Volume III* and *Lean Six Sigma Project Execution Guide* (Breyfogle 2010)
- Lean kaizen event: *IEE Volume III*, Section 36.9

14

BPM: Process Modeling

ABPMP BPM CBOK® description for process modeling is that the techniques combine a set of processes and skills which provide insight and understanding of business process and enable analysis, design, and performance measurements. Figure 12.1 illustrates where process modeling fits into the IEE BPM/EPM model.

14.1 Process Modeling and the IEE Value Chain

Models can be developed to support the organization's views for its enterprise, business, operations, workflow, systems, measurement, and control. The IEE value chain can be used as a readily available repository for accessing these various views of the organization.

In the IEE value chain, a:

- Process diagram can provide a simplified presentation of a process' basic work flow.
- Process map can provide more detail about not only the process but relationships to operators, events, etc.

- Value stream map can be used to analyze and design the flow of materials and information required to bring a product or service to a consumer.
- Process model can utilize more information to simulate the performance of a process.

In addition to providing linkage and integration of functional performance measurements, the IEE value chain provides a framework for documenting the business, operations, and technology domains of an organization, where each of these domains can be modeled. Among other things, these process models can:

- Increase understanding of how a process will perform under varying conditions. Improve insight to how a new process would perform before its implementation, perhaps identifying an unexpected problem which should be addressed before going live.
- Provide increased awareness of workflow bottlenecks and where improvement efforts should focus.

Observation, team meetings, and/or one-on-one discussions can be used for capturing information about a process.

Business Process Model Notation (BPMN) is a standard that provides a simple and robust modeling set of symbols for the various aspects of business processes. More information can be found at http://www.bpmn.org. The automation of a process can begin with a BPMN that describes the process; however, it is important to streamline a process as much as possible before its automation.

The IEE value chain can also provide a predictive measurement process performance, where these metrics can be updated automatically through EPRS software.

14.2 Process Simulation

Process simulations allow for mathematically examining how a process will perform under various scenarios. Simulations can be used to validate a new process model, predict how a process will perform under various situations, uncover which inputs affect process performance the most, and compare different process designs.

14.3 Additional Information

Illustration of an IEE value chain's:

- Process diagram with drill down: *IEE Volume II*, Figure 7.2
- Process diagram with swim lanes: *IEE Volume II*, Figure 7.3
- Value stream map: *IEE Volume II*, Figure 7.4

15

BPM: Process Design

The *ABPMP BPM CBOK*® states that "process design involves the creation of specifications for new and modified business processes within the context of business goals, process performance objectives, workflows, business applications, technology platforms, data resources, financial and operational controls, and integration with other internal and external processes. Both a logical design (i.e., what activities are performed) and a physical design (how the activities are performed) are included as deliverables."

Figure 12.1 graphically shows process design in the IEE BPM/EPM model.

15.1 Creating a New Process Model

New processes should involve executive leadership, process owners, and stakeholders. The process design team should include customers, operators, stakeholders, and subject matter experts.

Considerations when creating a new process should include:

- Standardization of processes.

- Targeting efficient achievement of desired process performance.
- Reduction of waste and maximizing use of value-added activities.
- Minimizing handoffs.
- Documenting process in a usable and easily accessible format.
- Determination of performance and control measurements that will be monitored.

Activities associated with process design should consider:

- Definition of process activities, rules, and handoffs.
- Conduct of process simulation and tests.
- Determination of how measurements and information will be captured and reported; i.e., as a 30,000-foot-level metric whenever possible.
- Formulation of an implementation plan.

Process designs should be aligned to overall business and customer needs. Businesses need to be willing to invest in process design not only in its initiation but in continuous improvement so that process efficiency improves.

16

BPM: Management Rules and IT Infrastructure

16.1 Management Rules

Management rules and policies need to be established and followed in any business. These rules provide guidance and constraints on business activities with a goal to ensure a consistency of behavior within an organization. Some of these rules are as simple as how often to report performance and who is needed to approve a purchase order, but these rules manage the routine activities throughout an organization.

A successful BPM implementation will have the applicable business and management rules codified or integrated into the processes. The real question to ask is which of the rules are applicable. Every organization has rules that are followed, of which many are documented rules, and some are informal or undocumented rules.

It can be difficult to identify the important business process rules from the less important rules during the analysis of a business process. In most business processes there are undocumented business rules that are very important, and there are documented business rules that are ignored because they are incorrect or just not important.

For this reason, a thorough analysis of the existing documented and undocumented rules should be completed before beginning to modify any existing business process. Consider the following questions about the business process rules:

- Why does the rule exist?
- Would removing the rule create problems?
- Should rules that are needed for special cases apply to all activities to keep it simple?
- Do the rules create unnecessary activities, approvals, or constraints on the process?
- If all of the rules are followed, will the business process result meet all expectations?
- Does the application of the rules remove a process flexibility that is truly needed to be successful?

Through an analysis of the business process and management rules, many organizations realize that some rules are outdated and that there are many beneficial rules that the workforce has developed. Your goal is to identify the minimum set of rules that will allow for a successful and compliant execution of the process. Try not to use this effort as a vehicle to introduce more rules.

16.2 IT Infrastructure

BPM is too often seen as an Information Technology's automation of processes. We need to consider IT as an enabler technology, not the driver of a BPM deployment. IT needs to provide information to the business in a format that is readily available so that the most appropriate decisions are made throughout the organization.

The IT infrastructure requirements vary based on the size of the BPM deployment (one location, multiple locations) along with the overall magnitude of the deployment of BPM. Many organizations by this time have a working data repository that is managed through an Enterprise Resource Planning (ERP) system, a Contact Relationship

Manager (CRM), or other data repository along with business process data residing on servers or PCs throughout the organization. A simple BPM effort that is applied to a single process may have a stand-alone IT infrastructure, but in every other case, the BPM infrastructure should be tied to or compatible with the existing data and information infrastructure existing within the organization.

This does not mean that an organization needs to transition to one of the big name data management systems before proceeding on the path towards a successful BPM deployment. The key is to have all of the data and process information that is collected from the BPM system available for performance reporting and analysis throughout the organization. This includes the transfer of data maintained on paper and worksheets into a data warehouse (database) where possible.

Selection of a BPM software design solution should be matched to the IT hardware available throughout the organization. An optimal balance of the BPM processing from local machines to servers can be quite dependent on the existing hardware or for a decision to distribute different hardware to each process location.

A centralized data repository for the ERP and BPM process data is preferred because it allows for a more powerful analysis of the business interactions and success drivers, but it is not necessary. Data linking across independent data sources can be accomplished, but it will introduce a bit more complexity into the analysis.

Consideration of the privacy and access control of both BPM process data and the business data that are associated with the process as well as user data should be considered. Integration of the BPM system into a single sign-in system, such as Active Directories, can simplify the access control if the organization has one in place.

17

Process Transformation

The *ABPMP BPM CBOK*® states "process transformation is the planned evolution of a business process using a clearly defined methodology and disciplined approach to ensure that the business process continues to meet business objectives."

17.1 How to Initiate Transformation

This book describes a methodology for achieving the above transformation objective. To illustrate this point, consider how:

- The IEE value chain provides
  - A vehicle for linking processes to their metrics, where, if the common-cause response of a process is undesirable, something different needs to be done within the process.
  - Readily available process and performance information that can be accessed by all who have authorization; e.g., using EPRS software.
  - Insight to what areas of the business need to be improved or automated so that the enterprise as a whole benefits.

  - A means to address cross-functional relations between people, processes, and technology.
  - A vehicle for communications among senior management, process owners, and those executing the details of the process.

- The EPM portion of IEE provides:
  - A systematic approach for making business risk analyses and management of those risks.
  - An effective methodology for leadership and Subject Matter Experts (SME's) for determining process improvement projects that have whole-system benefits through the blending of analytics with innovative thinking.
  - A means for senior management and process owners to be engaged, active, and visible for leading successful change.
  - An approach for the identification of processes that can be automated so that the enterprise as a whole benefits.

- The BPM portion of IEE provides:
  - An approach for managing operational metrics that have business controls.
  - A system for process modeling and simulation for the improvement and optimization of processes.
  - An integration of process automation into an encompassing business system.
  - The use of IT where there are whole enterprise benefits.

- Additional information about the IEE EPM/BPM system is available through the Smarter Solutions, Inc. website; e.g., http://www.smartersolutions.com addresses the following:

- *IEE Volume II* book provides details of the EPM portion of the IEE EPM/BPM system.
- *IEE Volume III* book provides details about executing an improvement project and process analysis for both strategically targeted and local improvement efforts.
- *Project Execution Guide* (Breyfogle 2010) provides a summary of the improvement project execution steps that are described in *IEE Volume III.*
- On-line and classroom training.
- An application discussion of this book's described techniques with a Smarter Solutions' team member.

18

Process Organization

18.1 Creating a Process Culture

Typically, management structure is function-based with a department hierarchy, where managers in this type of structure have responsibility for workers performing functional or resource tasks. These departments may be grouped by product, geography, or market, which can then lead to organizational silos as described in an organization chart. If care is not exercised, this form of structure can lead to competing organizational silo interests that could be detrimental to the enterprise as a whole.

Companies benefit when their organization has a process culture where business processes are known and visible to all employees, along with reporting of how the process, from a time-series measurement point of view, is performing over time. A process culture can be created through the use of an IEE value chain.

18.2 Process Management Roles

An individual may be responsible for one or more of the following roles, where organizations benefit when process information is made readily available through an organizational IEE value chain:

- **Process owners** are responsible for the execution and performance of an end-to-end process. Process owners also should be involved in the design and development of processes, where these processes are documented with their performance metrics in the IEE value chain. The process manager should also be involved in improvement efforts that are to enhance the process' performance.

- **Process improvement project managers** are individuals who have responsibility for improving process performance. These people could facilitate a Lean kaizen event, lead a Lean Six Sigma project, or execute a plan-do-check-act effort, all with the objective of improving work flow, reducing defect, costs, and/or efficiencies of a process that can impact its performance measurement.

- **Processes analysts** provide analyses of current processes, consider process design alternatives, and recommend alternatives. A process analyst effectively uses statistical techniques so that insight is gained into what might be done differently.

- **Process designers** are those who design new business processes, transform current business processes, and implement plans. Process designers ensure that process designs are in alignment and comply with the overall business needs.

- **Process architects** are responsible for the development, organization, and maintenance of a repository of standards relative to offered products/services, business processes, and performance measures. Business process architecture provides the foundation for analyses where opportunities can be identified for market advantage, business integration, and initiatives for internal processes.

Other key roles in process management include business analyst, subject matter experts, executive management/leadership, IT and other team members.

18.3 Organizational Structures

Organizations need to have a well-defined governance structure for leadership that clarifies decision rights, enabling the successful cross-functional and departmental process improvement efforts. This structure is what you see documented in an organizational chart and what is changed every time there is reorganization, even though the mission and the vision for the organization have not changed. For this reason, a Business Process Management implementation benefits when an Enterprise Process Management (EPM) function that is based on an organizational functional structure is included.

Benefits of this functional organizational structure include the following business and process management oversight benefits:

- The main business function management processes do not change with reorganizations.
- Performance metrics are consistent across all executions of the same function.
- Business management and process management rules do not change with reorganizations.

Organizations benefit from incorporating an Enterprise Process Management (EPM) function, which provides the oversight and resources for orchestrating and implementing the BPM/EPM components described in this book. Following the EPM guidelines, reorganization can change the reporting structure but not how the organization functions to meet its mission and vision.

19

BPM/EPM Technology

19.1 Application of BPM/EPM Technology

BPM/EPM technology application is effective with process complexity or when the amount of process information is too much for manual methods. The automation of workflows can highly enhance efficiencies through the reduction of time and costs of process activities. The caveat here is, of course, that automation efforts need to give focus to automation efforts where the expenditure of these resources most benefit the enterprise as a whole, as described in Section 9.4. Technology can also provide memory aids, balance workloads, and provide readily available information in processes.

BPM/EPM technologies can encompass process modeling, design, implementation, execution, monitoring, control, and performance analyses. Business process management suites (BPMS) can address needs such as documentation management, collaboration, workflow, routings, rules management, data warehousing, and communications management.

BPM/EPM technology can also provide the vehicle for creating and supplying IEE value chain information to those who have authorization throughout the organization. Through the EPRS system, both up-to-date performance measurements and their processes can be provided to those accessing the IEE value chain.

In addition, BPM/EPM technology can provide the means to capture and analyze data statistically so that insight can be gained to where improvement efforts should focus in making process improvement efforts.

20

Applying the IEE BPM/EPM Methodologies

20.1 Discovering Improvement Opportunities with Focused Status Meetings

There are many variations of the status meetings existing in organizations today. Some routine status meetings often discuss the problems of the day or week, where data may be presented as a stacked bar chart, pie chart or table of numbers. Most routine status meetings are disliked by all participants except the leader because they appear to have no benefits to the organization but are more of a complaint session. We have observed that this type of status meeting can lead to much firefighting rather than true process improvements.

A management-focused performance status meeting is a much better type of status meeting. In this meeting, the organizational performance is reviewed over time rather than just discussing the last period performance. This method ensures that all current performance data are considered in full context rather than just as a comparison to a goal. This difference may appear trivial, but it is truly significant.

In the IEE BPM/EPM model, the performance metrics are reported using an individuals chart format in order to evaluate the consistency or predictability of the process, and then the entire current period of consistency in the assessment of performance or capability is considered. It is the consideration of all performance data in the current period of consistency that keeps an organization from over-reacting or firefighting after observing every single bad performance value. The organization will act appropriately after a bad performance value if it is understood in context of the past performance history.

I have seen the dynamics of a status meeting completely change for the better when the organization's IEE value chain was viewed live through an Internet connection using a projector. When clicking through the IEE value chain during a meeting, 30,000-foot-level performance measures were examined and discussed. In one meeting, a functional manager stated that he thought one of his organization's tasks was a bottleneck that affected the whole site's throughput. His thought was that an improvement project was needed to determine what should be done differently to reduce the time it took to execute this task.

20.2 Where to Focus Our Enterprise Improvement Efforts and Process Automation

In a company, executives and management have been focusing their targeted improvement efforts and automation in areas that they thought would be aligned to their strategy. However, they noticed that these targeted projects often took a back burner to day-to-day events/crises and projects often seemed never to get completed on time or in a timely fashion, if they ever were completed. In addition, when projects were completed, often they did not have a positive financial impact.

To address this disconnect, the organization created an IEE EPM value chain. After an objective analysis of the enterprise as a whole, including the 30,000-foot-level IEE value chain dashboard metrics, it became obvious that focused operations improvement efforts should be redirected to improving the sales and marketing processes and automating the order-to-cash process (after it was improved).

Through analyses, it was determined that if the 30,000-foot-level metrics for each of these business processes improved, the financials would experience a positive gain. To ensure that the projects were completed on time, the owners of these processes were given the objective to improve their 30,000-foot-level metric's performance by twenty percent in eight months. Process owners were to report-out to executive management the status of the 30,000-foot-level metric that they were to improve and how the improvement project was progressing.

20.3 Reducing On-time Delivery Problems

A company was spending much money and resources expediting orders. This order-speed-up process was causing much organizational chaos, and the added shipping expense was hurting the bottom-line. Status meetings were focusing on resolving late-delivery problems instead of what could be done differently to prevent future late-delivery problems. The General Manager (GM) was frustrated and assigned Paula the project of determining what should be done to reduce the occurrence of this problem.

To resolve this process issue, Paula first wanted to quantify the severity of the problem. To do this, she created three 30,000-foot-level charts that quantified the following:

- Late-delivery frequency degraded to about 13% seventeen weeks ago.
- The proportion of shipments that were expedited was about 32%.
- The monthly expediting costs increased about seventeen weeks ago to an average of $38,400 per month.

Paula then did several statistical hypothesis tests of the late-delivery orders for the last seventeen weeks; i.e., the time since the late-delivery frequency degraded. From these analyses, Paula noted that most late-delivery orders were from one product line. Paula then worked with a team to create a value stream map of work flow in this product line.

From this map, Paula discovered that several people were not following a consistent process for one of the major steps in the value chain. These inconsistencies were leading to frequent rejections and rework, which added to processing delays. Paula worked with the team to document a new, enhanced consistent execution process.

From this work, Paula was able to demonstrate, through 30,000-foot-level reporting, the following:

- Late delivery frequency reduced from about 13% to 2%.
- The proportion of shipments that were expedited from about 32% to 3%.
- The monthly expediting costs decreased from about $38,400 to $500 per month.

Paula suggested to her GM that they also institute an IEE value chain with automatic updates so that everyone would have readily available access to both organizational procedures and 30,000-foot-level performance metrics. Paula explained to her GM that this form of reporting would, in addition to other benefits, be able to be used as a control mechanism to ensure that the processing would not transition back to its old ways; not only the process owner but the GM will have readily access to the performance reporting via a click of the mouse.

Paula's GM agreed to have her not only create the IEE value chain with automatic dashboard update reporting but also implement the IEE BPM/EPM system methodology.

20.4 Reducing Customer Service Return Call Rate

The manager of a customer service call center was concerned about the number of repeat calls that he was getting from customers because they did not get their issue resolved during their first conversation. This situation was adding to handling expense for each problem transaction and surely negatively impacting customer satisfaction. Because of this the customer service call manager assigned George the task of investigating the situation and reducing the repeat-call rate.

The first thing that George did was establish a baseline for the return-call rate. His 30,000-foot-level view of this metric indicated that approximately 37% of all calls resulted in a return call for the same issue.

Next, George conducted several statistical hypothesis tests. One test indicated that there was a statistical significant in frequencies of return calls by type of service. One type of service that the caller was inquiring about had a much larger frequency of calls than the other provided services.

George then analyzed the frequency of issues that call-ins had for the service which had the most inquiries. He noted that some types of issues had a much larger return-rate frequency. Paul then assembled a team which was familiar with the service offering and resolution process. Paul showed them the data and solicited what could be done to reduce the specific product's return-call rate. The team created a root-cause analysis tree, which could help the people taking the call to ask questions that would yield a quick determination of the most likely response for root-cause resolution.

George reported his findings to the customer service manager who had solicited his assistance. The customer service manager was pleased with the reduction in return calls from a rate of 37% to 4%. George also suggested that his organization also institute an IEE value chain with automatic updates so that everyone would have readily available access to both organizational procedures and 30,000-foot-level performance metrics.

George explained to the manager that this form of reporting would, in addition to other benefits, be able to be used as a control mechanism to ensure that the processing would not transition back to its old ways. Not only the process owner but the manager of this function will have ready access to the performance reporting via a click of the mouse.

The customer service manager got agreement from his peers and management to have George not only create the IEE value chain with automatic dashboard update reporting but also implement the IEE BPM/EPM system methodology.

20.5 Airport Parking Lot Could Benefit from BPM Simulation and VOC

A discussion with a shuttle bus driver when being recently transported to my car in my home town's airport highlights the importance of using business process management process simulation as a part of management's decision-making process. I will use the situation that we discussed in the shuttle bus to illustrate as a case study how organizations can save a great deal of money and avoid new-process-implementation risks, which can negatively impact the customer.

20.5.1 BPM System and Voice of the Customer

A few years ago, I became so frustrated with the parking process at the airport in the city where we live that I conveyed my complaint to the airport's parking lot management. The problem that I described to management was similar to what I have heard from others who used the parking lot; however, the airport's management ignored my complaint and simple-solution suggestion to their parking-lot issue.

Because my voice of the customer issue was not resolved, I now park my car, when traveling by airplane, in a privately-held remote lot, which accesses the airport through shuttle busses. The airport's on-site parking lot lost a customer because it did not consider my voice of the customer input.

Voice of the customer (VOC) is an important aspect of a Business Process Management System; however, organizations need to be aware that addressing VOC issues through process change can lead to unintended consequences.

20.5.2 Process Improvement Desire

The remote parking lot that I am now using has experienced such unintended consequence from a VOC improvement idea implementation. Why? The parking-lot company did not apparently conduct a BPM simulation to test a new process before going live.

To illustrate what happened, I will start by describing the remote-parking lot process before the change. This parking lot has rowed parking spaces, which are designated by a letter. Each space in the row has a number; hence a parking space might have a designation AA5; i.e., row AA and space 5 in row AA.

With the parking lot's initial process, the parking lot attendant would tell arriving drivers which lettered row that they were to enter to locate a space and park their car. Attendants assigned rows in the same general area to expedite the shuttle-bus loading process for travel to the airport so that travelers would not have delays in catching their flight.

After boarding, the shuttle driver would then write the lettered row and space number on a card and give it to each traveler upon boarding; i.e., to avoid the problem of people forgetting their space number when returning to pick up their car.

20.5.3 *Process Improvement Idea Implementation*

Management at the remote-parking lot had been receiving complaints about the lengthy time it was taking for customers to get to their car after returning from a trip. Management at the parking facility did listen to this VOC input and implemented a change, which was to reduce the amount of time it took for travelers to return to their cars' numbered space after completing their airplane travels.

The implemented improvement change was that, when a driver entered the parking lot to drop off a car, he was to indicate to the attendant what time of day he expected to return to pick up his car. The attendant would then assign the driver a letter which indicated a row that he was to park in. The idea was that people returning at a certain time of day would have their cars parked in a similar area, which would reduce the travel time for everyone in the shuttle bus to get to his car.

However, to implement this new process, two more shuttles and two additional drivers were needed to pick up the travelers after initially dropping off their cars. About 50% additional monthly miles were added to the shuttle fleet because more rows would need to be serviced for departing travelers. The expense to implement the change would be about $100,000 a year.

Because of this process change, voice of the customer inputs changed from some returning travelers' complaints about delays in getting to their cars to much customer outrage about the amount of time it was taking to get to the airport terminal for departing flights.

20.5.4 *BPM System Simulation and Risk Avoidance*

It is commendable that the remote-parking lot's management listened to Voice of the Customer (VOC); however, a BPM system simulation of the new process that they intended to implement would surely have identified the new issue that was encountered relative to customers' now having problems relative to getting to their flight departure gate in a timely fashion.

The remote-parking lot company would have saved much money and avoided customer outrage if only they had conducted a Business Process Management System simulation before making the process change. The simulation would have indicated that management should not implement the proposed change!

The shuttle driver told me that he expected that the company would be going back to their original process; however, before the company considers this, they should conduct a BPM simulation to determine what might be done to better serve the needs of both departing and returning customers.

20.5.5 *Additional Considerations*

What were described in this illustration are the benefits of one tool (i.e., simulation) in the overall IEE BPM/EPM roadmap. Additional company benefits could be gained if an organization were to evaluate and manage its enterprise as a whole using the IEE BPM/EPM system.

21

Applying IEE BPM/EPM Techniques to Your Situation

There is much discussion on the Internet and at conferences about selling BPM to others. What is needed is an approach which describes the benefits of the IEE BPM/EPM methodologies so that others can see not only the benefits of the approach but also how to get there.

This book chapter will describe how you could show the benefits, given various working environments.

In Section 1.1 you were asked to select which scenario most closely describes your situation. In this earlier section, I indicated that I would later share my thoughts on what could be the first steps of applying the concepts in this book to each scenario. Now is the time for giving my thought process.

21.1 New CEO to Revive Financials

You have been selected to revive the financials of a company as its new CEO. You are certain that the company's business management system needs to be improved, but you are not sure what would be the best alternative. Consider the following:

a. State to your executive team that you want to create a long-lasting IEE BPM/EPM system with their help. All members of the team are to read this book so that they understand toward what goal you will be moving the organization.

b. At the same time that the following steps are being conducted, you should plan to: learn what is currently occurring in the organization by walking around; attend executive, status and other meetings where you are only an observer; determine firsthand what your customer thinks by visiting a select few customers to have an honest one-on-one conversation.

c. Select a well-respected, system-thinking individual who will initiate and coordinate the following activities with a team that includes members of the executive team at various points in time; i.e., starting with the "d" activity.

d. Create the high-level functional categories of an IEE value chain by working not only with executives but also SMEs.

e. Agree to what would be good measures relative to quality, cost, and time for each IEE value-chain function. Place these metric categories in the IEE value chain.

f. Decide which performance measures in the IEE value chain would be the most important to provide insight into what is really occurring in the organization and what might be done differently; e.g., ten measures. Agree who will be the process manager who is responsible for each of these measures.

g. Decide how each of these measures will be tracked using a 30,000-foot-level dashboard approach.

h. Determine how performance data will be collected and stored for automatic-update reporting of each 30,000-foot-level metric in the IEE value chain; e.g., using IEE EPRS software.

i. Capture and report in the IEE value chain time-series data over the last two years, if possible, for each metric.

j. Have someone work with each process manager, who was assigned a key performance metric, to describe what occurs in his/her process from a high level point of view. Document this information in the IEE value chain.

k. Have someone conduct a quick overall analysis of the business. (See IEE Volume II Chapters 9 – 12)

l. At the end of the month, conduct a two-day executive retreat. During this retreat, among other things: the IEE value chain will be presented and collectively analyzed; an enterprise improvement plan (EIP) will be created with action plans; plans will be created for monitoring individual processes; next steps will be determined for adding to the IEE value chain and conducting follow-up meetings.

21.2 Executive That Finds Competition Eroding the Market

You are an executive who reports to the CEO of a company that is doing well; however, you are concerned that the competition may soon be eroding your market share. Consider the following:

a. You investigate to determine what your company should do differently from a process point of view and discover the IEE BPM/EPM system. You believe that this system is what you should incorporate in your company. The question is what you should do now to convince others.

b. There is someone who is a wizard at getting information and analyzing data who works in another's chain of command. You talk to the executive that you know has decision-making authority in his chain of command, asking if you could have her do some work for you. He says okay.

c. You ask the wizard to put a monthly estimate of where your company's market share was in a spreadsheet for the last five years.

d. After the wizard puts this data into a spreadsheet, you then ask her to investigate the 30,000-foot-level reporting methodology and then report the spreadsheet data in a 30,000-foot-level format.

e. Upon examining the market-share 30,000-foot-level performance metric, you note how your company's market share dropped significantly two months ago.

f. You ask your data wizard what happened during this time frame. She says that a competitor came out with a new product that had several benefits over your most popular product.

g. You set up a one-on-one meeting with your CEO to share the 30,000-foot-level market-share report-out. In your conversation with her, you make the point that, with your current performance reporting methodology, it would take a long time to note this problem.

h. You suggest that to resolve this immediate problem you need to expedite the development of a new product that is now in development.

i. You also suggest that you need to look into your entire process systematically. Using an IEE BPM/EPM approach, you believe that, if your team were to follow the IEE enterprise improvement process (EIP), you would conclude that your development process needs systematic re-examination to determine what you might do differently to expedite the process so that you better meet and exceed customer expectations. You state also that you believe a systematic investigation would uncover other process issues that you should work on; e.g., what should be done to reduce customer returns.

j. You state to the CEO that you believe the IEE BPM/EPM system is what your company should incorporate and suggest that she read this book. You suggest having a follow-up conversation in a week to discuss her thoughts about the IEE BPM/EPM system.

21.3 Your Company Has Declining Financials

You are working in a company that has declining financials, and you believe something different should be done in the business. Consider the following:

a. You record your organization's monthly profit margins for the last five years in a spreadsheet.

b. You report out these numbers in a satellite-level format, which is similar to 30,000-foot-level reporting, but satellite-level reporting is for financial metrics.

c. You are shocked to discover that profit margins were doing well until about eight months ago when they took a nose dive.

d. You ask your analytical friend what happened eight months ago. She does an investigation and notes that eight months ago your company's product return rate increased, and the amount of overtime pay was also increased to address these problems and to maintain timely completion of new orders.

e. You share this information with your boss. He is aware of the problem, but not the magnitude of the ongoing effect on the financials. He notes that the problem has been resolved for current-shipped product but there are still units in the field that will probably be returned in time. You state that you believe something different needs to be done not only for this current problem but also for how we examine processes and their metrics in general.

f. You suggest to your boss that your company should undertake an IEE BPM/EPM system. What you would like to do is present this problem and system alternative to a system-thinker influencer of the CEO.

g. Your boss agrees that such a meeting could be beneficial.

h. Your boss navigates the chain of command for a meeting with Sue, the company's chief financial officer (CFO) stating that there is an associate (i.e., you) who has some information that she should see. Your boss states to her that she might not later agree to do something different because of this meeting, which would mean that she wasted one hour of her life. However, on the other side of the coin, he believes that this could be one of the most beneficial hours that she spends for the company for the entire year. Sue agrees to meeting with you.

i. During a meeting in Sue's office, she agrees with the proposed methodology that you describe and sets up a meeting for you with the CEO, who also buys into initiating an IEE BPM/EPM system deployment.

j. The next steps that the CEO could follow are noted in item 1.

21.4 Your Company Is Doing Well but There Are Few Performance Measures

You are working in a company that is doing well, but there are few performance measures and standard operating procedures. Meetings don't seem to address the real issues, and things are chaotic. You believe that more systems and standard operating procedures are needed. Consider the following:

a. You recall that a 2009 *Economist* article, "Toyota: Losing its Shine" stated something that could be relevant to your situation. You find the article on the Internet (http://www.economist.com/node/15064411).

b. You print out the article and highlight the statement, "Mr. Toyoda had been reading *How the Mighty Fall*, a book by Jim Collins, an American management guru (Collins 2009). In it, Mr. Collins (best known for an earlier, more upbeat work, "Good to Great") describes the five stages through which a proud and thriving company passes on its way to becoming a basket-case. First comes hubris born of success; second, the undisciplined pursuit of more; third, denial of risk and peril;

fourth, grasping for salvation; and last, capitulation to irrelevance or death. Only 18 months ago Toyota displaced General Motors (GM), a fallen icon if ever there was one, as the world's biggest carmaker. But Mr. Toyoda claimed that the book described his own company's position. Toyota, he reckoned, had already passed through the first three stages of corporate decline and had reached the critical fourth."

c. You then ask yourself if your company is in stage three, headed for stage four. You conclude that the company is in this stage and that something needs to be done differently, now!

d. After investigating various alternatives, you conclude that if your organization implements an IEE BPM/EPM system, the issues that were described in Collin's book can be avoided.

e. You set up a meeting with your manager where you ask about any frustrations that she is having relative to what is occurring in the business. She responds that there seems to be much firefighting of the same issues, and things don't get completed in as timely a fashion as she thinks they should. You then show her the article "Toyota: Losing its Shine" and ask her what stage she thinks the company is in. She responds: stage three. You then ask her, if she were in charge of the company, would she think that something different should be done? She says yes. You respond, stating that you agree and suggest that she look into the IEE BPM/EPM system and give her a copy of this book. You then set up a follow-up meeting to discuss.

f. In your follow-up meeting with your manager, she points out that the company is large and there are several divisions. She states that she thinks that she could get the funds and resources to pilot the IEE BPM/EPM system in her area and then later show others what was done. You agree.

g. After the pilot IEE BPM/EPM system is up and running in your area of the business, it is noted that things are less chaotic, meetings are more efficient, and there is less firefighting common-cause variability as though it were special cause.

h. The results and details of implementing the IEE BPM/EPM system are shared with others higher in the organizational chart, which results in replication of the methodology in portions of the business.

21.5 You Are Chosen to Lead A New Process Improvement Function

Consider the following:

a. An Internet search indicates that individual Lean or Lean Six Sigma projects might appear beneficial, but are often in a silo where the enterprise as a whole does not experience the benefits. Because of this, Lean Six Sigma projects often don't get completed, and Lean Six Sigma deployments often stall out.

b. After further investigation, you uncover the IEE BPM/EPM system where improvement projects are selected so that there are whole enterprise benefits. In this system, an enterprise improvement plan (EIP) is created which results in performance measurement improvement needs pulling for projects that benefit the enterprise as a whole. The added benefit of this approach is that process owners/managers are asking for timely completion of improvement projects in their area since they understand that this work is essential for their measurement to improve. These process managers will have a sense of urgency since every month they will be reporting to their leadership the status of their metric, which the project's completion is to improve.

c. You decide to implement your Lean Six Sigma deployment around the IEE EPM process for project selection, thinking that you will later suggest to your leadership that they consider the entire IEE BPM/EPM system.

21.6 You Have Been Selected to Lead a BPM Deployment

Consider the following:

a. You purchase the Association of Business Process Management Professionals (ABPMP) book titled *Guide to the Business Process Management Common Body of Knowledge (ABPMP BPM CBOK®)*.

b. You noted how the *ABPMP BPM CBOK®* contains much information about what should be included in BPM; however, the book does not describe a detailed roadmap for implementing BPM.

c. You note from an Internet search that many providers of BPM are focusing on the automation of processes; however, you think that there should be more to a BPM deployment.

d. Another Internet search uncovers the IEE BPM/EPM system for implementing BPM. You decide to use this approach for implementing BPM, following the steps noted in number one of this sequence of illustrations.

21.7 Your BPM Deployment Is Focused on IT Solutions and Missing the Management System

Your BPM deployment is focusing first on process automation; however, you believe that more can be done with the management system's supporting the BPM deployment so that the overall financials benefit. Consider the following:

a. An Internet search uncovers the IEE BPM/EPM system for implementing BPM.

b. You decide to set up a meeting with the leader of your BPM deployment, Sam. In your meeting with Sam, you ask him to share his thoughts about your current BPM implementation. He states that he thinks that some processes initially were automated that were helpful to the business financials but now it seems like there is automation of processes, which takes much resource effort, that do not have much impact on the overall organizational financials. You then say that you agree and think that the organization needs to have more in the BPM deployment than just automation. You mention that the Association of Business Process Management Professionals (ABPMP) book titled *Guide to the Business Process Management Common Body of Knowledge (ABPMP BPM CBOK®)* discusses much more than automation for a BPM deployment.

c. In your meeting with Sam, you suggest that he look over the *ABPMP BPM CBOK®* and also the IEE BPM/EPM system described in this book. You plan for having a meeting next week to discuss.

d. In your next meeting with Sam, he states that he agrees with your thoughts and will present to his leadership that the current BPM approach migrate to an IEE BPM/EPM methodology.

22

Achieving *ABPMP BPM CBOK®* Critical Success Factors

IEE BPM/EPM provides a system for achieving all of the following listed *ABPMP BPM CBOK®* critical items, as noted below:

- "Alignment of business strategy, value-chain definitions, and business processes."

  The EPM portion of the IEE BPM/EPM system describes linkage of strategy with the IEE value chain.

- "Establishment of enterprise and business goals to meet business strategy."

  Enterprise and business goals are established and aligned with business strategy through creation of the IEE enterprise improvement plan (EIP).

- "Development of action plans and business tactics to successfully meet the organization's goals."

  An EIP leads to the creation of targeted business objectives and tactics that benefit the enterprise as a whole. For detailed process improvement and project execution, IEE BPM/EPM roadmaps provide guidance for the facilitation of completion of action plans for successful achievement of these goals.

- "Assignment of executive sponsorship, responsibility, authority, and accountability for processes leading to attainment of goals."

  Through an EIP, high potential areas at the executive level are identified for improvement opportunities so that the enterprise as a whole benefits. Executives who are accountable for each of these business areas are responsible to enhance the key metrics that impact these high potential areas. Executives accomplish this objective by working with process owners on improvement efforts in their areas to enhance these key performance measurements.

- "Assignment of clear process ownership along with authority to engineer change."

  The IEE value chain can provide organizational 30,000-foot-level performance metrics, which can be updated automatically by using EPRS software, for example. Each of these metrics is to have a process owner who is responsible for providing acceptable performance from his process. When improvement goals are established for a process metric, the business and process owner are responsible for initiating the effort and providing the resources needed to achieve significant enough process improvement that established goals are achieved.

- "Establish metrics, measure and monitor process"

  The IEE BPM/EPM system provides a roadmap for the establishment of long-lasting metrics for all functions relative to quality, cost, and time. These metrics can be tracked using a predictive dashboard system that can be updated automatically through EPRS software so that measurement performance can quickly be assessed.

- "Institutionalize practices such as continuous improvement investigations, change management, change controls, and proper leverage of BPM products and tools that lead to improvements and change."

  The IEE BPM/EPM system provides a systematic approach with applicable tool sets for analyzing systems and determining where and how improvement efforts would be most beneficial.

- "Standardize and automate business processes and related methodologies across the enterprise."

  The IEE BPM/EPM system's value chain provides a vehicle for determining the standardizing of processes that can be shared across the enterprise. In addition, this system provides the means to determine where the automation of business processes is most beneficial.

23

Business Process Management Self-Assessment and Next Steps

Table 23.1 can be used for a self-assessment of an organization's maturity relative to implementing BPM/EPM. The lowest score for all categories can be used to quantify the maturity that an organization has. Categories with the lowest scores are opportunities for improvement.

23.1 Next Steps

I hope that this book has given you some ideas on what you might do either to initiate or enhance your organizational BPM effort. I hope that you also have gained some ideas on what you might do to create an organizational process-based system that breaks down silos, is data driven, and eliminates playing games with the numbers.

Table 23.1: Criteria for a self-assessment of an organization's BPM/EPM maturity

Business System Maturity	EPM/BPM based Business System in Place	Process aligned metric usage	Predictive performance reporting	Automation in reporting	Decisions based on performance metrics	Entire enterprise linked through a single reporting system	Strategies developed from performance gaps	Strategic alignment of improvement efforts
10	EPM/BPM part of the culture	100%	100%	100%	100%	100%	100%	100%
9	90%	100%	100%	80%	85%	100%	100%	85%
8	80%	100%	85%	60%	70%	85%	100%	70%
7	70%	100%	70%	40%	55%	70%	80%	55%
6	55%	100%	55%	20%	40%	55%	60%	40%
5	40%	80%	40%	few	25%	40%	40%	25%
4	25%	60%	25%	few	10%	25%	20%	10%
3	10%	40%	10%	few	few	10%	Some	Some
2	5%	20%	few	few	few	few	Some	Some
1	No uniform business system	few	few	few	few	few	Some	Some

In this book, I have described an entire BPM/EPM system. You may feel overwhelmed and say that this BPM approach is too much to undertake. With the end-in-mind system that I have been describing in this book, you can shrink the change to something that can be more bite-size for a start. You can then later build upon this foundation at whatever speed you want. For example:

- You might want to evaluate your current metric reporting to see whether the resulting actions from these reports lead to the most appropriate actions. To do this, you could compare, for a few metrics, a 30,000-foot-level report-out to your current report-out. From this comparison, did your current report-outs lead to firefighting common-cause variability as though it were special cause? If so, the result of this comparison work could lead to an improved measurement-reporting structure in your BPM deployment that is quite beneficial. One manufacturing company in Germany changed in its manufacturing operations to a 30,000-foot-level reporting structure because common-cause variability had been reported as special cause with its previous system.
- Another thing that you might want to do to enhance a BPM deployment is to build an IEE value chain for your area with linkage to the big picture. From this work, you could then link key metrics to this value chain, where there is a 30,000-foot-level reporting for the selected performance measurements. You might want to also include your current reporting methodology in the value chain so that others can readily compare the actions that could come from each of the reports.
- If you are having difficulties getting improvement efforts completed in your BPM deployment, you could build an EIP with existing projects on the right side of the figure to see how much alignment there is between the projects and the organization's current strategy and financials. If there is not much alignment, this could result in a change in the process for determining where to focus improve efforts and how to align this work with operational value-chain metrics, which is what this book suggests.

I hope that these scenarios have given you some ideas of things you can do immediately. If you have any questions about application of the described methodologies to your situation or need any help getting started with utilizing the orchestrated BPM system described in this book, contact us at Smarter Solutions, Inc. through forrest@smartersolutions.com, info@smarterolutions.com, or +1 512.918.0280. Many descriptive articles, blogs, videos, and recorded webinars, which you could find very helpful, are also available through our website, www.smartersolutions.com.

Besides general questions about application of the techniques to a specific situation, Smarter Solutions can help:

- Facilitate organizational IEE value chain creation with its predictive performance metrics.
- Provide automation of IEE value chain performance measurement reporting through use of EPRS software, https://www.smartersolutions.com/software/eprs-server
- Provide facilitation and training in the creation of an EPM system, which leads to process improvement efforts so that the enterprise as a whole benefits.
- Provide training and coaching in BPM tools and methodologies.
- Provide training and coaching on the execution of effective process improvement efforts that follow a detailed project execution roadmap, which is described in our books.

Wishing you the best in your journey!

Acronyms and Glossary

Acronyms

BOK	Body of knowledge
BPM	Business process management
BPMN	Business Process Model Notation
CL	Centerline of a control chart
CODND	Cost of doing nothing differently
DFA	Design for assembly (Example of DFX)
DFM	Design for manufacturability (Example of DFX)
DFX	Design for X or a characteristic; e.g., DFA or DFM
DMAIC	Define-measure-analyze-improve-control
DOE	Design of experiments
DPMO	Defects per million opportunities
EIP	Enterprise improvement plan
EPM	Enterprise process management
EPRS	Enterprise performance reporting system (software)
ERP	Enterprise process resource planning
5S	Sorting, Storage, Shining, Standardize, Sustaining
FT	Fault tree
Hyp	Hypothesis
KPI	Key performance indicator
IEE	Integrated Enterprise (process) Excellence
LCL	Lower control limit
LSS	Lean Six Sigma
MBA	Master of business administration

PDCA	Plan-do-check-act
RCA	Root cause analysis
SMART	Specific, measurable, actionable, relevant, time-based
SME	Subject matter expert
SPC	Statistical process control
30k	30,000-foot-level
TOC	Theory of constraints
TPS	Toyota production system
TQM	Total quality management
UCL	Upper control limit
VOC	Voice of the customer
WIP	Work in progress, Work in process

Glossary

IEE Volume III and/or *IEE Volume II* provide the details of executing the tools described in this Glossary.

Analysis of means (ANOM): A statistical procedure to compare the means of individual groups to the grand mean.

Balanced scorecard (the): The balanced scorecard (Kaplan and Norton 1992) tracks business organizational functions in the areas of financial, customer, and internal business process and learning & growth. In this system, an organization's vision and strategy also lead to the cascading of objectives, measures, targets, and initiatives throughout the organization. For issues with this approach see *IEE Volume II,* Section 3.6.

Baseline: Beginning information from which a response change is assessed.

Bottleneck: The slowest operation in a chain of operations; it will pace the output of the entire line.

Bottom line: The final profit or loss that a company experiences at the end of a given period of time.

Brainstorming: Consensus-building among experts about a problem or issue using group discussion.

Common cause: Natural or random variation that is inherent in a process over time, affecting every outcome of the process. If a process is in-control, it has only common-cause variation and can be said to be predictable. When a process experiences common-cause variability but does not meet customer needs, it can be said that the process is not capable. Process or input variable change is needed to improve this situation; i.e., this metric is creating a pull for project creation.

Control chart: A procedure used to track a process with time for the purpose of determining if common or special causes exist.

Control: The term in-control or predictable is used in process control charting to describe when the process indicates that there are no special causes. Out-of-control indicates that there is a special cause or that the process is unpredictable.

Cost of doing nothing differently (CODND): The direct and indirect costs associated with the current process; e.g., cost of current levels of WIP and all generated costs from defective units.

Customer: Someone for whom work or a service is performed. The end user of a product is a customer of the employees within a company that manufactures the product. There are also internal customers in a company. When an employee does work or performs a service for someone else in the company, the person who receives this work is a customer of this employee.

Cycle Time: Frequency that a part/product is completed by process. Also, time it takes for operator to go through work activities before repeating the activities. In addition, cycle time can be used to quantify customer order to delivery time.

Dashboard: See Scorecard.

Defect: A nonconformity or departure of a quality characteristic from its intended level or state.

Defective: A nonconforming item that contains at least one defect or a combination of several imperfections, causing the unit not to satisfy intended requirements.

Deming, Dr. W, Edwards: As an American statistician, Dr. Deming is known for his top-management teachings in Japan after World War II. Dr. Deming made a significant contribution to Japan's becoming renowned for its high-quality, innovative products.

DMAIC: Define-measure-analyze-improve-control Six Sigma roadmap.

Dot plot: A plot of symbols that represent individual observations from a batch of data.

DPMO: When using the non-conformance rate calculation of defects per million opportunities (DPMO), you need first to describe what the opportunities for defects are in the process; e.g., the number of components and solder joints when manufacturing printed circuit boards. Next, the number of defects is periodically divided by the number of opportunities to determine the DMPO rate.

Drill down: To drill down is to transition from general category information to more specific details by moving through a hierarchy.

Enterprise improvement plan (EIP): A project drill-down strategy that follows: goal—strategies—high potential area—projects.

Enterprise process management (EPM): Rather than having a governance model that addresses initiatives as separate entities, in IEE a value chain EPM function can be created that orchestrates this system. The EPM function is responsible for integrating, overseeing, and improving the execution of these processes, utilizing an IEE BPM/EPM roadmap.

EPM: See Enterprise process management.

Enterprise Performance Reporting System (EPRS): Software that provides up-to-date performance measurement and procedural reporting throughout the organization, where measurements have a 30,000-foot-level and satellite reporting that can provide predictive statements.

Failure: A device is said to fail when it no longer performs its intended function satisfactorily.

Failure rate: Failures/unit time or failures/units of usage. Sample failure rates are 0.002 failures/hour, 0.0003 failures/auto miles traveled, 0.01 failures/1000 parts manufactured.

Fault tree analysis: A schematic picture of possible failure modes and associated probabilities.

5S: Method that focuses on improvements through sorting (cleaning up), storage (organizing), shining (cleaning), standardize (standardizing), and sustaining (training and discipline).

50-foot-level: Low-level tracking of a key process input variable; e.g., process temperature when manufacturing plastic parts or daily sales person activity. This type of chart can involve frequent sampling to make sure that the desired input level is maintained over time. Tracking at the 50-foot-level can lead to the timely detection and resolution of problems or undesirable drifts in input levels so that the 30,000-foot-level metric for product/service quality, timeliness, and other metrics is not jeopardized.

Firefighting: The practice of giving much focus to fixing the problems of the day/week. The usual corrective actions taken in firefighting, such as tweaking a stable/predictable process, do not create any long-term fixes and may actually cause process degradation.

Governance, corporate: The system by which business corporations are directed and controlled. The corporate governance structure specifies the distribution of rights and responsibilities among different participants in the corporation, such as the board, managers, shareholders and other stakeholders, and spells out the rules and procedures for making decisions on corporate affairs. This system also provides the structure through which the company objectives are set and the means of attaining those objectives and monitoring performance. – Organization for Economic Cooperation and Development (OECD)

Hoshin kanri: Japanese name for policy deployment. Used by some Lean companies to guide their operations strategy. For issues with this approach see *IEE Volume II,* Section 3.5.

Hypothesis: A tentative statement, which has a possible explanation for some event or phenomenon. Hypotheses are not theoretical statements. Instead, hypotheses have a testable statement, which might include a prediction.

Hypothesis test: Consists of a null hypothesis (H0) and alternative hypothesis (Ha) where, for example, a null hypothesis indicates equality between two process outputs, and an alternative hypothesis indicates non-equality. Through a hypothesis test, a decision is made whether to reject a null hypothesis or not. When a null hypothesis is rejected, there is risk of error. Most typically, there is no risk assignment when we fail to reject the null hypothesis. However, an appropriate sample size could be determined so that failure to reject the null hypothesis is made with risk of error.

IEE: See Integrated Enterprise Excellence.

IEE Value chain: Describes in flowchart fashion both primary and support organizational activities and their accompanying 30,000-foot-level or satellite-level metrics, which can provide predictive statements. An example of primary activity flow is: develop product—market product—sell product—produce product—invoice/collect payments—report satellite-level metrics. Examples of support activities include IT, finance, HR, labor relations, safety & environment, and legal. An organizational IEE value chain can be provided automatic metric updates through Enterprise Performance Reporting System (EPRS) software.

In control: The description of a process where variation is consistent over time; i.e., only common causes exist. The process is predictable.

IT: See Information technology.

Kaizen: Continuous incremental improvement

Kaizen event or blitz: An intense short-term project that gives focus to improve a process. Substantial resources are committed during this event; e.g., Operators, Engineering, Maintenance, and others are available for immediate action. A facilitator directs the event, which usually includes training followed by analysis, design, and area rearrangement.

Lean: Improving operations and the supply chain with an emphasis on the reduction of wasteful activities such as waiting, transportation, material hand-offs, inventory, and overproduction.

Lean Six Sigma: A process improvement methodology that follows a define-measure-analyze-improve-control (DMAIC) roadmap for the execution of improvement projects.

Lead time: Time for one piece to move through a process or a value stream. Lean time can also describe the setup time to start a process.

Mean: The mean of a sample is the sum of all the responses divided by the sample size. The mean of a population is the sum of all responses of the population divided by the population size. In a random sample of a population, the mean of the sample is an estimate of the mean of the population.

Metric: a measurement that quantifies a particular characteristic.

Nonconformance: Failure to meet specification requirement.

Normal distribution: A bell-shaped distribution that is often useful to describe various physical, mechanical, electrical, and chemical properties.

Null hypothesis: See Hypothesis testing.

Out of Control: Control charts exhibit special-cause(s) conditions. The process is not predictable.

Pareto chart: A graphical technique used to quantify problems so that effort can be expended in fixing the "vital few" causes, as opposed to the "trivial many." Pareto chart is named after Vilfredo Pareto, an Italian economist.

Plan-do-check-act (PDCA): Frequently referred to as the Deming cycle or Shewhart cycle. Sometimes the check step is replaced with a study step; i.e., PDSA. PDCA has the following components: Plan – Recognize a need for change, then establish objectives and process for delivering desired results; Do – Implement change that is to be assessed; Check – study results and identify lessons learned; Act – Use lessons learned to take appropriate action. If change was not satisfactory, repeat the process.

Porter's value chain: In 1985 Michael Porter described the value chain in his book *Competitive Advantage: Creating and Sustaining Superior Performance* [Porter 1985]. Porter's value chain is a sequence of activities an organization performs in order to deliver a valuable product or service for the market.

Predictable: The control limits in a control chart are calculated from the data. Specifications in no way affect the control limits. This chart is a statement of the voice of the process (VOP) relative to whether the process is considered in statistical control or not; i.e., stable/predictable or not. Since people often have difficulty in understanding what in control means, I prefer to use the term predictable instead of in control.

Predictable process: A stable, controlled process where variation in outputs is only caused by natural or random variation in the inputs or in the process itself.

Probability plot: Data are plotted on a selected probability paper coordinate system to determine if a particular distribution is appropriate (i.e., the data plot as a straight line) and to make statements about percentiles of the population. The plot can be used to make prediction statements about stable/predictable processes. *IEE Volume III* describes the creation of this plot.

Problem (solving): The process of determining the cause from a symptom and then choosing an action to improve a process or product.

Process: A method to make or do something that involves a number of steps. A process can be primary/core, support, or management.

Process performance metric: IEE uses the term process performance metric to describe a process's predictive output in terms that everyone can understand. The process to determine this metric is: 1. An infrequent subgrouping/sampling plan is determined so that the typical variability from process input factors occurs between subgroups, e.g., subgroup by day, week, or month. 2. The process is analyzed for predictability using a 30,000-foot-level control chart. 3. For the region of predictability, the non-compliant proportion or parts per million (ppm) are estimated and reported. If there are no specifications, the estimated median response and 80% frequency of occurrence are reported.

Process diagram: Path of steps of work used to produce or do something.

Pull: A Lean term that results in an activity when a customer or down-stream process step requests the activity. A homebuilder that builds houses only when an agreement is reached on the sale of the house is using a pull system.

Push: A Lean term that results in an activity that a customer or down-stream process step has not specifically requested. This activity can create excessive waste and/or inventory. A homebuilder that builds houses on the speculation of sale is using a push system. If the house does not sell promptly upon completion, the homebuilder has created excess inventory for his company, which can be very costly. See pull.

Random: Having no specific pattern.

Root cause analysis: A study to determine the reason for a process nonconformance. Removal or correction of the root cause eliminates future nonconformance from this source.

Sample: A selection of items from a population.

Satellite-level: Used to describe a high-level IEE business metric that has infrequent subgrouping/sampling so that short-term variations, which are caused by typical variation from key process input variables, will result in control charts that view these perturbations as common-cause variability. This metric has no calendar boundaries and the latest region of stability can be used to provide a predictive statement for the future.

Scorecard: A scorecard helps manage an organization's performance through the optimization and alignment of organizational units, business processes, and individuals. A scorecard can also provide goals and targets, which helps individuals understand their organizational contribution. Scorecards span the operational, tactical, and strategic business aspects and decisions. A dashboard displays information so that an enterprise can be run effectively. A dashboard organizes and presents information in a format that is easy to read and to interpret. In this series of volumes, I make reference to the IEE performance measurement as either a scorecard or scorecard/dashboard.

Significance: A statistical statement indicating that the level of a factor causes a difference in a response with a certain degree of risk of being in error.

Six Sigma: A term coined by Motorola that emphasizes the improvement of processes for the purpose of reducing variability and making general improvements.

SMART goals: Not everyone uses the same letter descriptors for SMART. My preferred descriptors are italicized in the following list: S - specific, significant, stretching; M - measurable, meaningful, motivational; A - agreed upon, attainable, achievable, acceptable, action-oriented, actionable; R - realistic, relevant, reasonable, rewarding, results-oriented; T - time-based, timely, tangible, trackable.

Soft skills: A person who effectively facilitates meetings and works well with other people has good soft skills.

Special cause: Variation in a process from a cause that is not an inherent part of that process. That is, it is not a common cause.

Specification: A criterion that is to be met by a part or product.

Stability: Refers to both statistical stability of measurement process and measurement stability over time. Both are vital for a measurement system to be adequate for its intended purpose. Statistical stability implies a predictable, underlying measurement process operating within common-cause variation.

Stakeholders: Those people or organizations who are not directly involved with project work but are affected its success or can influence its results. Example: stakeholders are process owners, managers affected by the project, and people who work in the studied process. Stakeholders also include internal departments which support the process, finance, suppliers, and customers.

SWOT: Analysis used in strategic planning to determine organizational strengths, weaknesses, opportunities, and threats.

Theory of constraints (TOC): As described in *The Goal* (Goldratt 1992), constraints can be broadly classified as being internal resource, market, or policy. The outputs of a system are a function of the whole system, not just individual processes. System performance is a function of how well constraints are identified and managed. When we view our system as a whole, we realize that the output is a function of the weakest link. The weakest link of the system is the constraint. If care is not exercised, we can be focusing on a subsystem that, even though improved, does not impact the overall system output. We need to focus on the orchestration of efforts so that we optimize the overall system, not individual pieces. Unfortunately, organizational charts lead to workflow by function, which can result in competing forces within the organization. With TOC, systems are viewed as a whole and work activities are directed so that the whole system performance measures are improved.

Three Rs of business: Everyone doing the right things and doing them right at the right time.

30,000-foot-level: A process response that is used in IEE to describe a high-level project or operation metric that has infrequent subgrouping/sampling so that short-term variations, which might be caused by input random perturbations, will result in charts that view this variability as common cause. It is not the intent of the 30,000-foot-level control chart to provide timely feedback for process intervention and correction, as traditional control charts do. Example: 30,000-foot-level metrics are lead time, inventory, defective rates, and a critical part dimension. There can be a drill down to a 20,000-foot-level metric if there is an alignment; e.g., the largest product defect type. A 30,000-foot-level individuals control chart can reduce the amount of firefighting in an organization when used to report operational metrics. As a business metric, 30,000-foot-level reporting can lead to more efficient resource utilization and less playing games with the numbers.

TOC: See Theory of constraints.

Total quality management (TQM): A management program which worked on continuous product/service improvements through workforce involvement.

Toyota production system (TPS): Toyota developed techniques that focus on adding value and reducing waste through setup, lead time, and lot size reduction. The term has become synonymous with Lean manufacturing.

TQM: See Total quality management.

Value-added (VA) time: The execution time for the work elements for which a customer is willing to pay.

Value stream mapping (VSM): At Toyota, value stream mapping is known as "material and information flow mapping." In the Toyota production system, current and future states/ideal states are depicted by practitioners when they are developing plans to install Lean systems. Infinite attention is given to establishing flow, eliminating waste, and adding value. Toyota views manufacturing flow as material, information, and people/process. The described value stream mapping covers the first two of these three items (Rother and Shook 1999).

Voice of the customer (VOC): The identification and prioritization of true customer needs and requirements, which can be accomplished through focus groups, interviews, data analyses, and other methods.

Waste: Seven elements to consider for the elimination of muda, a Japanese term for waste, are correction, overproduction, processing, conveyance, inventory, motion, and waiting.

WIP: A general description for inventory that is being processed within an operation or is awaiting another operation.

Work in process (WIP): See WIP.

References

Shortcut References throughout Book

ABPMP BPM CBOK®: Association of Business Process Management Professionals (2009), *Guide to the Business Process Management Common Body of Knowledge*, Version 2.0, Association of Business Process Management Professionals.

IEE Volume II: Breyfogle, F. W. (2008a), *Integrated Enterprise Excellence Volume II - Business Deployment: A Leaders' Guide for Going Beyond Lean Six Sigma and the Balanced Scorecard*, Bridgeway Books. For more details and discount purchasing see https://www.smartersolutions.com/books/.

IEE Volume III: Breyfogle, F. W. (2008b), *Integrated Enterprise Excellence Volume III - Improvement Project Execution: A Management and Black Belt Guide for Going Beyond Lean Six Sigma and the Balanced Scorecard*, Bridgeway Books. For more details and discount purchasing see https://www.smartersolutions.com/books/.

Additional References

Breyfogle, F. W. (2008c), *The Integrated Enterprise Excellence System: An Enhanced, Unified Approach to Balanced Scorecards, Strategic Planning, and Business Improvement*, Bridgeway Books.

Breyfogle, F. W. (2008d), *Integrated Enterprise Excellence Volume I - The Basics: Golfing Buddies Go Beyond Lean Six Sigma and the Balanced Scorecard*, Bridgeway Books.

Breyfogle, F. W. (2010), *Lean Six Sigma Project Execution Guide: The Integrated Enterprise Excellence (IEE) Process Improvement Project Roadmap*, Citius Publishing.

Collins, J., Porras, J., (2004) *Built to Last: Successful Habits of Visionary Companies*, HarperCollins.

Collins, J., (2009) *How The Mighty Fall: And Why Some Companies Never Give In,* HarperCollins.

Covey, S. (2004), *The 7 Habits of Highly Effective People: Powerful Lessons in Personal Change*, Simon and Schuster.

Deming, W. E. (1986), *Out of the Crisis*, MIT Press.

Dodd, C.W., (1992), Design for `X', IEEE Potentials, October, pp. 44-46.

Goldratt, E. M. and Cox, J, (1992), *The Goal: A Process of Ongoing Improvement*, North River Press.

Hambrick D. C. and Fredrickson J. W. (2001), "Are you sure you have a strategy?" *Academy of Management Executive*, Vol. 15, no. 4.

Kaplan, R. S. and Norton, D. P. (1992), "The Balanced Scorecard – Measures that Drive Performance," *Harvard Business Review*, Jan.-Feb.

Kohlbacher, M. (2009), "The Effects of Process Orientation on Customer Satisfaction, Product Quality and Time-Based Performance," Paper presented at the 29th International Conference of the Strategic Management Society, Washington DC, October 11–14.

Porter, M., (1985), Competitive Advantage: Creating and Sustaining Superior Performance, Free Press.

Rother, M. and Shook, J. (1999), *Learning to See: Value Stream Mapping to Add Value and Eliminate MUDA*, Lean Enterprise Institute, Inc.

Scheer, A.W. (2007) Professor Scheer's Advanced BPM Assessment, IDS Scheer AG.

Thiault, Dominique (2012), "Managing Performance through Business Processes: From BPM to the Practice of Process Management," CreateSpace Independent Publishing Platform.

Index